此书为 2018 年浙江省金华市文化扶持项目成果

金华文化双语读本

李慧　主编

吉林大学出版社

图书在版编目（CIP）数据

金华文化双语读本：汉英对照 / 李慧主编 . ——长春：
吉林大学出版社，2019.1
ISBN 978-7-5692-4399-4

Ⅰ . ①金… Ⅱ . ①李… Ⅲ . ①文化史—金华—汉、英
Ⅳ . ① K295.53

中国版本图书馆 CIP 数据核字 (2019) 第 042915 号

书　　　名：金华文化双语读本：汉英对照

作　　　者：李　慧　主编
策划编辑：朱　进
责任编辑：朱　进
责任校对：冯莉娜
装帧设计：张玲燕
出版发行：吉林大学出版社
社　　　址：长春市人民大街 4059 号
邮政编码：130021
发行电话：0431-89580028/29/21
网　　　址：http://www.jlup.com.cn
电子邮箱：jdcbs@jlu.edu.cn
印　　　刷：三河市嵩川印刷有限公司
开　　　本：787mm×1092mm　　1/16
印　　　张：11.25
字　　　数：200 千字
版　　　次：2019 年 1 月第 1 版
印　　　次：2023 年 9 月第 3 次
书　　　号：ISBN 978-7-5692-4399-4
定　　　价：36.00 元

《金华文化双语读本》编委会

顾　问：吴远龙　宓智瑛　徐玉书

　　　　徐　卫　许　倩　Arthur

主　编：李　慧

副主编：王　芳　许　倩

编　委：曹艳梅　蒋中意　李　倩

　　　　梁　妍　童小婉

前　言

　　"为什么我的眼里常含泪水，因为我对这土地爱得深沉"——艾青。

　　——这也是我们编译此书的初心。

　　金华，古称婺州，素有"小邹鲁"之称，又因地处金星与婺女星争辉之处而得名。金华历史悠久，名人辈出，物产丰富，景色宜人。金华人包容开放，既注重创新又重视文化传承；金华婺学兼容并蓄，影响深远；金华婺商开拓进取，携手共进；金华工艺美妙绝伦，享誉中外；金华婺剧既古老优雅，亦鲜明生动；金华景观人文与自然融合恰当，沁心宜人。

　　金华，美而悠久，丽而卓远。

　　作为金华人，我们肩负着继承和传播金华的责任和义务；作为地方高校教师，我们应主动承担文化传承的任务，为推动本地文化建设做出应有的贡献。

　　本书汇集编译团队三年的地方文化实践教学宣讲成果，以金华文化为内容，以双语的形式介绍金华文化，包括历史沿革、地质地貌、行政区域、金华名人、婺学、婺商、婺剧、金华民俗、金华特产、金华景观等。其中值得一提的是，将婺学、婺商、婺剧写入双语，也将历史传承与现代文化编入读本，既有历史的沉淀，又富含现代光辉。本书的编写是团队智慧的结晶，但是受于能力和水平的因素，书中定有不当和不妥，甚至错误之处，恳请读者批评指正。并希望此书的出版能够为金华文化双向传播做出贡献。

编　者
2018 年 8 月

序

　　由李慧主编，王芳、许倩两位同志为副主编的《金华文化双语读本》即将出版，请我为序，感到十分荣幸和高兴。现竭诚向读者推荐。自从"中国十佳宜居城市"排行榜设立以来，金华已9次荣登榜位。这个素有"历史文化之邦、山清水秀之乡"美称的城市，近几年随着一带一路、浙中城市群、金义都市区的建设，更是迎来了千载难逢的发展机遇。为什么金华能成为浙江省内的第四大都市区，为什么市政府下大决心作出战略决策，提出构筑综合交通廊道、金义科创廊道和浙中生态廊道三条廊道，打造都市区同心圆，要支撑起浙中金华的崛起之梦？我想，读者看完这本《金华文化双语读本》，您一定能从历史文化的角度静悟体味到其中缘故。近年来，金华外事办和侨办组织的多次外国名校学子进古村活动，不少外国学子提出要把金华的故事讲到世界上去。所以，编写一本《金华文化双语读本》具有极其重要的现实和长远意义。

　　人类有文字的历史只有五千年，我们金华有婺城的历史就有两千多年。如何编辑一本反映金华文化与自然遗产的书籍，不仅能荟萃早在南宋时期诗人李清照笔下金华的"水通南国三千里，气压江城十四州"的文明菁华，揭示出金华各个历史时期促进多元文化的碰撞与交流，同时将分散的、相互隔绝的地域链接，融合为一个整体，一个统一的光环带，来展示金华源远流长的人类社会进步和发展的风貌，显然并非易事。

　　为此，李慧主编带领她的团队，以镜头式的方式加以浓缩，呈现一个纵向或横向的展开，以达到全方位传播历史文化知识的目的。本书不追求将某些具有传奇色彩的传说编成吸引读者以吸引读者眼球的故事，而是努力争取给予读者提供某些具有永恒价值的知识，激发读者对自身周围环境的发展有所发现、有所认识；激活和深化读者对这些文化遗产与当今家国情怀相连的社会生产生活的关系的理性思维，从而领悟到政治、经济、宗教、民俗文化、地方文化和民族文化乃至与国际关系等因素的相互影响。

　　本书内容章节清晰可见，恕不赘述。本人只想再次郑重向大家推荐，本书内涵丰富，包含极其珍贵文化信息，对讲好金华文明发展故事，对推动目前爱家乡、爱金华，建设好金华，无疑是为读者打开了一个全景式浓缩下来的窗口。凭此窗口可扩大我们的地理视野，进一步探索未知领域，拓展我们今天的活动与金华的生存空间。以李慧为首的编写和教学实践团队，无疑为金华做了一件大有裨益的好事。我热切地希望编者们本书发行之后，要及时收集读者反馈意见和建议，编写团队的眼光始终追随着探索的步履，随着更多金华文化遗产的发现和确认，不断融合进新东西，使本书有动态性地升华与完善。

　　是为序。

宓智瑛

目 录

第一章　金华

Chapter One Jinhua

第一节　简介[①] Profile

金华位于中国的东南沿海的一个美丽而富饶的省份——浙江省。金华为省辖地级市,下辖婺城和金东两区,义乌、东阳、兰溪、永康四市,以及潘安、浦江和武义三县。面积为 101918 平方千米。界于北纬 28° 32'～29° 41' ,东经 119° 14'～120° 46' 之间,东邻台州,南毗丽水,西连衢州,北接绍兴、杭州。年平均气温 17.3℃～18.2℃。全年总降水量在 1109.0～1305.2 毫米之间。6 月初进入梅汛期,降雨连续时间较长,但降雨总量和强度不大。年日照时数 1528.8～1808.9 小时。

Jinhua City, located in southeast coastal area of China, belongs to Zhejiang Province, beautiful and rich. It is a prefecture-level city of the province with two districts: Wucheng and Jindong, four county-level cities (Dongyang, Yiwu, Lanxi and Yongkang) and three counties (Pan'an, Pujiang and Wuyi). The whole city occupies an area of 10918 square kilometers. Jinhua is located at 28° 32'-29° 41' N, 119° 14'-120° 46' E. It borders Taizhou in the east, Lishui in the south, Quzhou in the west, Hangzhou and Shaoxing in the north, the annual average temperature is

17.3℃~18.2℃, and the annual rainfall ranges from 1109.0 millimeters to 1305.2 millimeters. The Meiyu period is in early June, with a relative long period of rainfall but without large total rainfall and high intensity. The annual average sunshine is 1528.8−1808.9 hours.

金华古称"婺城",因其地处婺女与金星两星争华之处而得名。自秦王政 25 年(公元前 225 年)建县至今已有 2200 多年的历史。金华在历史上一直是浙江中西部的中心城市,曾经管辖 26 个县。"水通南国三千里,气压江城十四州",这是南宋诗人李清照客居金华时所写的诗句。她生动地概括了金华重要的地理位置和金华城雄伟的气势。金华拥有悠久的历史和灿烂的文化。金华素有"小邹鲁"之称。历代名人辈出,文坛巨匠、爱国人士、专家学者、丹青大师,金华概不乏人。

Jinhua is called Wuzhou in ancient times, a name based on a legend that it was the place where the Venus Star and the Wunv Star scrambled for being magnificent. It has been over 2200 years since the time when the Emperor Qin set up the county of Jinhua in his 25th year of the empire (225 B.C.). Jinhua was always the central city in the mid-west of Zhejiang Province and had ever 26 counties under its jurisdiction in the history. "The water route covers thousands of *li* to the south states, and the momentum overwhelms dozens of counties of the river city" is a verse written by Li Qingzhao, a known woman poet in the Southern Song Dynasty when she stayed in Jinhua. She vividly epitomized the important geographical location and the magnificent momentum of Jinhua City. Jinhua has a long history with a glorious and splendid culture. It is commonly known as "Xiao Zoulu", where distinguished people emerged in large numbers. You can find literary giants, patriots, experts and scholars, painting masters emerging in almost each dynasty in Jinhua.

金华历来是浙江的教育之邦,自古教育兴盛。历史上学术繁荣、书院层出不穷。数以万计的学生学业有成,散布海内外。金华具有悠久的历史和深厚的民族文化底蕴。诗词戏曲辈出杰作,文章书画代有人家。金华戏曲源远流长,有 400 多年历史的婺剧是金华历史文化中的一朵奇葩。1962 年,浙江婺剧团进京演出的《断桥》被周恩来总理誉为天下第一桥。金华婺剧曲径通幽,民间文化更是丰富多彩。金华斗牛是一种带有东方独特魅力的民间娱乐活动,其风情可与西班牙斗牛相媲美,被称为"东方一绝"。金华斗牛已受邀赴杭州、上海等地表演。所到之处,观者如云。除了斗牛,舞龙灯、迎大旗、永康十八蝴蝶等,各具特色,引人入胜。

Jinhua has also been a "City of Education". Education here has been encouraged and flourished since the ancient times. In the city, systematic learning was prosperous and academies sprung up in the history. Hundreds and thousands of students here have successfully completed their course study, and now work and study at home and abroad. Jinhua has long been the representative of historical trends and has profound national culture. Known poems, verses and traditional operas came out in large numbers, and masters in literary works, paintings and calligraphy can be found in almost every generation. Jinhua operas can be dated back to ancient times. The Wu Opera with a history over 400 years is an exotic flower in the garden of literature and arts in Jinhua, Zhejiang Wu Opera Troup went to Beijing in 1962 to perform the opera "Broken Bridge", which was acclaimed by our former premier Zhou Enlai as "the First Bridge on Earth". Wu Opera is profoundly performed in a simple way, while other local others are also diverse and stunning. Jinhua bull-fighting is a kind of folk amusement with unique eastern charm. Its performance can be well matched with that of Spanish bull-fighting. That is why it is called "A Unique in the East". Nowadays, Jinhua bull-fighting has been performed in some other places such as Hangzhou, Shanghai, etc. Wherever it goes, hundreds of spectators will gather to enjoy watching it. Apart from the bull-fighting, playing dragon lanterns, Pan' an Election of a Great Flag Pole and Yongkang "Eighteen Butterflies" have their own features. They are wonderful and fascinating.

金华气候温和,雨量充分,土地肥沃,物产富饶。金华的花茶,举岩茶和佛手均闻名于国内。金华特产当中,火腿独具盛名。金华火腿形似琵琶,皮薄,骨细,肉色红润,香气扑鼻,美味可口。素以"色香味形"四绝闻名,曾在国内外博览会上多次获奖。金华酥饼表里香脆,内蕴外酥,油而不腻。金华传统手工艺术百花齐放。东阳木雕和竹编、浦江草编和水晶、永康五金等历史悠久,其产品畅销海内外。

Jinhua is characterized by temperate climate, plentiful rain, fertile land and abundant products. Scented tea, Juyan tea and finger citron tea are all famous. Among all the local products, Jinhua ham surely comes out first. Like *pipa* in appearance, Jinhua ham has thin-skin and soft-bone, tender meat, which is fragrant and tasteful. It is known at home and abroad for its "Four Specials" of color, smell, taste and formation. Jinhua ham has won several gold awards in many domestic and international fairs. Jinhua Subing is a kind of cake with a special flavor, characterized by being crispy outside with rich taste inside. It is fatty but not so greasy, tasty and preservable. Traditional handicrafts have been flourishing in Jinhua. The wood carving and bamboo weaving in Dongyang, the straw plaiting and crystals carving in Pujiang, and hardware crafts in Yongkang, all enjoy a long history of development, and the products sell well both at home and abroad.

金华栽种茶花的历史有 800 多年。在 1986 年十月第一届市人代大会上,茶花被誉为金华市市花。1999 年,金华市政府决定举办国际茶花大会。2002 年 12 月 26 日,金华与欧洲客商签订了 1000 万元茶花标准苗的订单。2003 年举办了国际茶花大会。11 万株经过检疫的茶花和月季等标准苗运至"世界花木之都",自此金华茶花成功进入欧洲市场。

The history of growing camellia in Jinhua has been at least over 800 years up to now. The first session of the city's People's Congress held in October of 1986 decided to name the flower as the City Flower. In 1999, the city government decided to take bids for the next International Camellia Conference. On 26th of December, 2002, Jinhua signed an order form for standard camellia young plants valued at ten millon yuan with travelling traders from European countries. Then it held the 2003 International Camellia Conference. 110,000 quarantined camellia and standard rose young plants were sent to "The World Flowers Metropolis". Jinhua camellia successfully entered European markets for the first time.

金华属丘陵盆地地貌,属于亚热带季风气候。自然风光极富特色,境内山川秀丽,河谷众多。丘陵延绵,峰岭挺拔。其中以双龙五洞十景和兰溪六洞构成的溶洞群竞相争奇,以方岩山、九峰山为代表的丹霞地貌挺拔俊秀;以婺江、兰溪江为代表的江河风光旖旎,以金华北山国家级森林公园为代表的山林景观一派郁郁葱葱。除此之外,金华还有很多奇观美景,比如浦江仙华山、武义郭洞、东阳三度等。

With a hilly and basin landform and subtropical monsoon climate, Jinhua's natural landscapes is varied and distinctive. It has rich resources in natural sceneries such as beautiful monutains and waters, crisscrossed river valleys, precipitous rides and peaks. Among all the landscapes, the most attractive are the carst-cave groups represented by the five caves and ten sights of the Double-dragon Cave as well as Lanxia Liudong; the magnificent and charming Danxia landform represented by the Fangyan and the Jiufeng Mountains; the picturesque scenery of rivers and lakes represented by Wujiang River and Lanxi Rivers. You will find a vast area of lush and green wooded mountains represented by Beishan State-level Forest Park. Apart from the above mentioned, there are also many wonderful places in various parts of Jinhua, such as the Xianhua Mountain of Pujiang, Guodong of Wuyi and Sandu of Dongyang.

金华自然景观丰富,寺庙楼阁林立、名胜古迹众多。金华拥有国家级文保五处,最值得一提的是太平天国侍王府,是我国目前保存原貌最完整、规划艺术最丰富、建筑规模最大的太平天国遗址。金华人文景观丰富,位于东阳的横店影视城以华夏五千年为主线,先后建起了 8 个拍摄基地。

Jinhua is rich in natural landscapes. Here you can find a lot of temples and pavilions, numerous scenic spots and historical sites. The city has five state-level historical sites under national protection. Among all these historical sites, the one worth mentioning is Shi Wang Fu, a historical remain of the Taiping Heavenly Kingdom, which is the most well preserved and the largest construction site with rich design arts. Jinhua is also rich in humanistic landscape. Hengdian Film and Television Base located in Dongyang City which has a 5000-years Chinese history as the main line has set up eight shooting scenes one after another.

金华拥有先进的民营企业。金华主导产业有服装和纺织、机械和电子、制药和化工、制造工艺、金属加工、建筑和建材、汽车和摩托车配件、食品加工和塑料器皿等。各县市乡镇特色产业分布因地制宜。比如,义乌小商品、永康汽车摩托车配件以及机械电子、东阳服装建筑和磁性材料、兰溪有色金属、毛巾、日化、浦江纺织、制锁和水晶产品等。

Jinhua has advanced private economy. Leading industries of the city include clothing and textile, mechanics and electronics, pharmacy and chemistry, manufacturing crafts, metalwork processing, architecture and building materials, automobile-and-motorcycle accessories, food processing, and plastic ware, etc. Industries are distributed with typicall characteristics in different counties or county-level cities. For instance, Yiwu is characterized by its light-industry commodities, Yongkang by its automobile-and-motorcycle accessories and mechanical and electric tools, Dongyang by its clothing, architecture and magnetic materials, Lanxi by its non-ferrous metal, cement, towels and daily chemicals, and Pujiang by its textile, lock making, and crystals, etc.

金华市交通便捷,是中国东南沿海和陆地的重要交流中心,也是国家陆地运输的主要交通枢纽之一。对外形成了铁路、公路、水路和航空的综合运输网络。沪昆铁路、金千铁路和金温铁路在金华市交汇。杭长高铁、新金温高铁已建成并运营。市域内公路通车里程达 4739 千米,金华公路北通杭州、上海,西连衢州,东接宁波、台州港口,南达温州港。沪昆高速

第一章 金华 Chapter One Jinhua

公路、甬金高速公路、长深高速公路、台金高速公路、诸永高速公路等8条高速公路贯穿金华。金华距离上海自驾约三小时,高铁约一个半小时,普通列车约四个小时。义乌机场先后开通的航线有北京、上海、广州、深圳、厦门、青岛、香港等二十多条。

Jinhua is a substantial exchange center with convenient transportation in the coastal and inland areas of the Southest China. It is one of the major hubs of landway transportation in the country. There is a strong com-prehensive transportation network with railways, expressways, waterways and airways. The Shanghai-Kunming railway, Jinhua-Qiandaohu railway, Jinhua-Wenzhou railway intersect in Jinhua. Hangzhou-Changsha High-speed railway and Jinwen High-speed railway have been in use. It has 4739 km-long traffic mileage, connecting Hangzhou and Shanghai in the north, Quzhou in the west, Ningbo and Taizhou ports in the east, and reaching Wenzhou port in the south. Eight express highways including Hukun Highway, Yongjin Highway, Changshen Highway, Taijin Highway, Zhuyong Highway and others-run through the city. Jinhua is approximately three hours' drive to Shanghai. There is also the G-train (Gaotie, high-speed train) that takes approximately 1.5 hours. It is about four hours by ordinary train. Yiwu Airport offers airlines to more than twenty cities including Beijing, Shanghai, Guangzhou, Shenzhen, Xiamen, Qingdao and Hong Kong.

金华不断完善基础投资环境。在各个工业园区,都以高标准基础设施进行设置。基本达到供水、供电、道路、燃气、供热、排水排污、网络通信等。从政府官员到普通市民,都树立招生引资、对外开放的意识。

Jinhua has constantly improved its basic investment environment. In all the industrial gardens, the basic facilities have been installed at a high standard. On the whole, they have met the requirement of water, electricity, gas and heat being supplied, drainage, postal and telecommunications, cable television and land being leveled, etc. They call for all people, from government officials to ordinary citizens, to foster the idea of opening to the outside world.

走在这民间小路，我们感受这巍巍北山的古老和浑厚，踏过这景观大道，我们融入这城市跳动的节奏。远处，斗牛场中传来的号角声穿过我们的耳畔，近郊，茶花园里溢出的清香触动着我们的心田。眼前，城市中的异彩纷呈撩开了我们的眼帘，明日的金华正吸引着五湖四海的来客。如今，新时代为金华带来了新的历史机遇，金华的明天必将更加辉煌灿烂。

Strolling on the small road in the forest, we are affected by the old age, simplicity and honesty of the majestic North Mountain; while we walking through the Jingguan Grand Road, we seem to be merged into the beating rhyme of the city. In the distance, the horn sounding in the bull-fighting field comes up to our ears, while in the suburbs, the fragrance spilling out from the camellia gardens sweetens our hearts. Before our eyes, the radiant splendor in the city strikes our heartstring. The charming Jinhua is attracting more and more visitors from all corners of the land. Now the new century has brought about a new chance for this city. It is certain that tomorrow's Jinhua will be more brilliant and magnificent.

第二节　金华历史　Jinhua History

金华古称婺州，文化历史悠久，名人辈出，被誉为"小邹鲁"。

Jinhua, known as "Wuzhou" in ancient times, with a long history with celebrities coming forth, is honored "Xiao Zoulu".

一、上山文化　Shangshan Culture

金华有人类生活与文化创造的历史，最早可追溯到一万多年前的上山文化。上山文化居民是最早从山地穴居到河谷平原定居的人群之一。他们打制石器与磨制石器并存，具有明显的由旧石器向新石器过渡的特征。上山人使用陶器作为日用器具。在晚期上山文化遗址中发现彩陶，彩陶上面太阳纹图案以及遗址中发现的祭祀坑表明上山人已经开始了信仰生活。采集、渔猎和种植水稻是他们获得食物的主要方式。

The earliest history of human life and culture creation could date back to Shangshan Culture, about more than ten thousand years ago. The habitats of Shangshan Culture settled down from mountains to valleys and plains. The fact that they ground and polished stones is an obvious characteristic during the transition from the Paleolithic Age to the Neolithic Age. Shangshan People used potteries as daily ware. The painted potteries with sun patterns and the sacrifice pits found in the late Shangshan Culture relics indicate that Shangshan People have already had beliefs. They mainly live on collecting, fishing and hunting, planting rice.

上山文化距今 11400—8500 年，是迄今为止长江中下游地区发现的最早的新石器时代文化。上山文化不仅是金华走向文明的开端，也拉开了浙江新石器文化的帷幕。上山文化后，在钱塘江两岸发展出不同的新石器文化系列。从考古材料看，跨湖桥文化、河姆渡文化和良渚文化都在这片土地上打下了深深的烙印。

Shangshan Culture dating back to about 8,500 to 11,400 years ago was the earliest discovered culture of the new Neolithic Age in the middle and lower reaches of the Yang tze River. Shangshan Culture not only starts the civilization of Jinhua but also launches the Neolithic Culture in Zhejiang. From Shangshan Culture, a series of Neolithic cultures derive, including Kuahuqiao culture, Hemudu Culture and Liangzhu Culture, which have profound influence on this land.

二、於越姑蔑 —— 先秦时期的金华 Pre-Qin Jinhua: Wuyue Gumie People

古越人是对长江中下游地区各部族人的统称。印纹陶、青铜工具和土墩墓是古越人突出的物质文化特征。他们在生存与发展的过程中还形成了许多与中原不同的文化特点与风俗。古越人善舟船，是舟船的初创者，并且有着凿齿、断发、文身的习俗。先秦时期生活在金衢盆地的居民属於越人,是广布东南沿海的百越部族中最古老和最发达的一支。於越人不仅建立了国家,而且在春秋晚期一度拥有霸主的地位。

Guyue People, the general designation for the tribes at the middle and lower reaches of the Yangtze River, are culturally characterized by impressed potteries, bronze tools and mounded tombs. They developed various cultures and customs, compared with those in the central plains. In particular, Guyue People, the first skilled boat-makers, were featured with a custom of chiseled teeth, broken hair and tattoos. The Pre-Qin habitats in Jin-Qu Basin were Yuyue People, who were the most ancient but most developed group among Baiyu tribes along the southeast coast of Guang Dong. Yuyue People not only established a country but even had supreme reign over others in the late Spring and Autumn Period.

姑蔑国　Gumie Kingdom

在春秋战国时代,除了古越人,在今汤溪一带还生活着从北方迁徙过来的姑蔑族。姑蔑本是黄河流域的一个古老国族。周初东征践奄,姑蔑作为被征服国族,一部分留居鲁地逐渐融入华夏,其主体部分则辗转南下到达越国,并在越国的军事政治活动中发挥过重要影响。地理位置大概在今天的金华汤溪、兰溪西乡与衢州境。

Besides Guyue People, Gumie families immigrating from the north lived in the place of Tangxi named for today during the Spring and Autumn period and the Warring States period. Gumie is an ancient tribe along the Yellow River. In the early Zhou Period, Gumie was conquered, a small part of them stayed in the Lu State and gradually merged into Huaxia, while the majority, together with other ethnic groups, went southward to the Yue State where they played an important role in military and politics. The Gumie State was located in the present Tangxi, Xixiang of Lanxi and Quzhou.

三、秦汉六朝时期的金华　Jinhua in the Qin-Han and the Six Dynasties

设县置郡　Establishment of Prefectures and Counties

公元前221年，秦始皇统一中国后，实行郡县制，在全国设三十六郡，郡以下设县，今义乌稠城为中心置乌伤县，属会稽郡。这是金华最早的行政建制。东汉初平三年，在乌伤县西部立长山县，辖今金华市婺城区、金东区和兰溪市全境。到了汉末，将西部都尉治所迁至长山县。三国时期，以长山县为中心设立东阳郡，并兴建子城。在南朝时期，将东阳郡更名为金华郡。

The first emperor of Qin unified China in 221 B.C., and established prefectures and counties. There were 36 prefectures superior to counties. The present Choucheng of Yiwu was the central Wushang County, belonging to Kuaiji Prefecture, which was the earliest administration system in Jinhua. In the third year of the Chuping Period of the Eastern Han Dynasty, Changshan County established in the west of Wushang County ruled over the present Wucheng District, Jindong District and Lanxi City in Jinhua. At the end of the Han Dynasty, the west administrative seats of the military officer were moved to Changshan County. In the Three Kingdoms Period, Dongyang Prefecture, taking Changshan County as its center, was established with defensive Zicheng. During the Southern Dynasties, Dongyang Prefecture was renamed as Jinhua Prefecture.

筑堰制瓷　Dams and Ceramics

秦汉帝国的重心在中原地区，江南地区较少受到关注，经济处于低迷状态。到汉末三国时期，随着政治格局的变化，一些基础性的建设开始启动，为农业经济的发展奠定了基础。金衢盆地东部地形起伏较大，水系贯穿其间，使此地成为水旱灾害较严重的地区之一。民间依靠自己的力量，根据山形水势筑造堰坝，引水灌溉，大大促进了农业的发展。与此同时，手工制造业也有进步，青铜冶炼兴起，制瓷业更是蓬勃发展，其中，化妆土的应用和堆塑艺术的成熟是陶瓷烧造工艺的重要突破。

The central plains were the core of the Qin-Han Dynasties, while the southern area with a stagnant economy was seldom concerned. Till the Three Kingdoms period in the last few years of the Han Dynasty, with the adjustment of political patterns, it started the basic construction to pave a foundation for developing agricultural economy. Flood and draught hit the eastern Qin-Qu Basin severely, for its great topographic relief with rivers running through. The local folks basing on mountains and rivers established dams for irrigation, which greatly accelerated the development of agriculture. Meanwhile, the handicraft manufacturing also took a further step, the bronze melting flourished, while the porcelain production blossomed, too. In particular, the application of engobe and the maturity of relief decoration were major breakthroughs in the ceramics-firing process.

崇佛兴道 Worship of Buddhism and Prosperity of Taoism

佛教大约在汉末三国时期开始传入金华一带。金华最早的佛寺是三国孙权时期的东阳法兴寺，南北朝时期又建造了北山的智者寺。南北朝时期还流行着嵩头陀达摩到金华建寺传教的故事。相传在嵩头陀达摩的影响下，傅翕开创了儒释道"三教合一"的中国维摩禅，推动了佛教汉化的进程。在道教方面，出现了风靡华南的黄大仙信仰，对后世产生了重大的影响。如今的黄大仙信仰已经超脱普通宗教意义而成为世界华人对祖国情感的共同维系。

Buddhism was introduced to Jinhua in the Three Kingdoms Period in the last years of the Eastern Han Dynasty. The Faxing Temple was the earliest one in Jinhua during Sunquan-ruling period, while the Zhizhe Temple was built in Beishan in the Northern and Southern Dynasties when the legend of the Buddhist master's giving lectures was spreading over. According to the legend, under the influence of the master, Fuxi initiated the Chinese Weimo dhyana *zen*, an integrated belief of three religions, which promoted a Chinese-featured Buddhism. As for Taoism, the faith of Huang Daxian sweeping southern China had a significant impact on aftertime. The faith at present has developed much more meaning rather than being a religion, and has became the deep rooted sentiment of the Chinese towards their homeland.

文教之风　Culture and Education

伴随早期的经济开发，加上中原文化的影响，金华的文化教育活动开始发展起来。两晋时期有两位出色的太守诗人，他们不仅用自己清新的诗风突破了空谈玄理的玄言诗，还为金华的文化生活抹上了文学与诗歌的色彩，尤其是沈约的八咏诗，为金华的文化打下了恒久的印记。这一时期，授徒讲学之风也开始兴起，刘峻筑室紫岩洞，徐伯珍讲学于九峰，为金华日后繁荣的书院文化奠定了坚实基础。

With the early economic development and impact from the central-plain culture, the culture and education in Jinhua started to develop. During the Jin Dynasties, there were two outstanding poets who not only took their fresh poems to break through the metaphysical poetry featured in metaphysics but also colored Jinhua culture and life with literature and poetry, of which in particular, the Eight - Chant Poems of Shenyue laid a permanent mark on Jinhua culture. In this period, recruiting students and lecturing began to be popular: Liujun built a learning room in Ziyan Cave, Xu Bozhen lectured in Jiufeng, which laid a solid foundation for the upcoming prosperous academy culture.

四、隋唐宋元时期的金华　Jinhua in the Sui, Tang, Song and Yuan Dynasties.

金华经历多次郡州变革，终于在唐武德四年以州的建制确立，定名"婺州"。唐末五代，在吴越王钱镠辖下，社会经济有所发展，居民的活动范围也进一步拓展，婺州在子城之外兴建罗城，取代了子城的军事防御功能。两宋时期是金华经济、社会、文化的全面发展时期，不仅创烧出婺州窑乳浊釉瓷，还因发达的水路和繁荣的经济面貌而备受世人关注，尤其是宋室南渡后定都临安,金华因地近京畿而达官显贵聚集,南宋时期婺州人进士有 478 位,其中四位作为丞相,问鼎政界。当时有许多名门望族到金华定居,使金华成为名副其实的南宋重地。

Jinhua going through multiple administrative reforms, was finalized as "Wuzhou (Wu State)" in the fourth year of Wu De in the Tang Dynasty. During the late Tang and Five Dynasties, under the governance of Emperor Qianliu of Wuyue, the society and economy developed, and the living areas for habitats expanded in Wuzhou, Luocheng was set up around Zicheng and substituted Zicheng in military defence. The society, economy and culture developed comprehensively during the two Song Dynasties when the opacifier glazed porcelains of Wuzhou kilns came out, and the advanced waterways and prosperous economy drew worldwide attention. Being close to the capital, there gathered dignitaries after the Song royals went southward and settled down in Lin'an. Particularly, in the Southern Song Dynasty, there were 478 *jinshi* scholars, four of whom were prime ministers in governmental circles. What's more, a number of notable families settled in Jinhua and made Jinhua an important place at that time.

经历秦汉至六朝时期的初步开发,金华的社会经济摆脱了早期的低迷状态,进入较快速的增长时期。手工业呈现初步的繁荣,尤其引人注目的是制瓷业的发展。婺州窑源起于东汉末年,是唐代汉族制瓷名窑,以青瓷为主,在唐代以茶碗盛名,及至隋唐,婺州窑成功创烧出乳浊釉瓷,进入五代、北宋,其精品堪与越窑、瓯窑媲美,尤其是堆塑工艺,达到了很高的水准,在宋元时期作为外销瓷销往海外。南宋时期,金华深受南宋建都临安的影响和辐射,城乡经济进一步发展,尤其是水陆交通的发达,金华婺江两岸出现繁华市景,布庄与绸庄、酒肆、火腿铺、金华酥饼店、茶铺在当时发展迅速。

After the preliminary development from Qin-Han to the Six Dynasties, Jinhua got rid of the early economic downturn and stepped into a quite rapid-growth period. The handicraft industry showed a preliminary prosperity development, and the porcelain industry especially caught attention of the public. Wuzhou prodution, originated in the late East Han Dynasty, was famous among Han people for its kiln of porcetains in the Tang Dynasty. The porcelains were mainly green ones in quality, and tea bowls thrived in the Tang Dynasty. Up to the Sui and Tang Dynasties, Wuzhou Kiln successfully produced opacifier glazed porcelains, and the fine products could match those produced in Yue Kiln and Ou Kiln in the Five Dynasties and the Northern Song Dynasty. What's more, the techniques of modeling stereoscopic patterns or images on porcelains had reached a high level. These porcelains were sold into markets abroad during the Song and Yuan Dynasties. The urban and rural economy in Jinhua developed further, because the capital was moved to Lin'an in the Southern Song Dynasty. The well-developed waterways and land transportation made the city prosperous on both sides of rivers. Besides, cloth and silk stores, wine shops, ham shops, Jinhua crispy cake shops as well as tea houses grew rapidly at that time.

儒风佛韵　Confucianism and Buddhism

随着社会经济的开发，金华的文化出现了新一轮的发展。文学、哲学与宗教呈现出新的气象。唐代婺州诗人张志和以一曲《渔歌子》唱尽江南美景，成为历代“渔歌”范本；万佛塔平地崛起，精美的塔身与地宫精致的供养见证了佛教的昌盛；在哲学方面，南宋时期浙东学派异军突起，其中以吕祖谦的金华学派、陈亮的永康学派构成的婺学最盛。及至元代，何基、王柏、金履祥、许谦“北山四先生”承袭朱学，促使婺学与文学合流。

In pace with the social and economic development, the culture of Jinhua greeted a new development, and the literature, philosophy and religion also took on a new look. *The Fishing Song* written by Zhang Zhihe, a poet of Wuzhou in the Tang Dynasty, depicted a complete charming scenery along the lower reaches of the Changjiang River, and has become a model for later versions. The Wanfo Pagoda with elegant body and fancy underground palace witnessed the prosperity of Buddhism. As for philosophy, the Zhedong school emerged all of a sudden, among which, Lv Zuqian of Jinhua school and Chenliang of Yongkang school composed the best Wu Learning. Up to the Yuan Dynasty, He ji, Wang Bai, Jin Lvxiang and Xu Qian known as "the Four Beishan Philosophers" followed Zhu Xi's theory, and integrated Wu Learning with literature.

五、明清时期的金华　Jinhua in the Ming and Qing Dynasties

浙江之心　The Center of Zhejiang

　　元末明初，朱元璋率部从皖入浙，攻占婺州，改名为宁越府，誉之为"浙江之心"。朱元璋吸收了包括宋濂、王祎在内的大批文人志士，加速了统一全国的步伐。明成化七年（1471年），宁越府改金华府，辖领八县，"八婺大地"成为金华的代名词。抗倭是明代政治的重要内容，义乌兵成为戚继光军的主要力量，南征北战，留下不朽功绩。明末清初，婺州朱大典、张国维抗清守婺以身殉国。正因为婺州人不屈的抗争精神，清政府加强了婺州的驻军数量以保证政局稳定。清末，太平天国侍王李世贤以金华为浙江的起义指挥中心，建造了规模宏大的侍王府，为金华历史留下了浓重的一笔。

　　During the period of the late Yuan Dynasty and early Ming Dynasty, Zhu Yuanzhang marched from Wan(Anhui) to Zhe(Zhejiang) and conquered Wuzhou, he renamed Wuzhou to Ningyue Prefecture which was honored as "The Heart of Zhejiang". In order to accelerate unificayiog the nation, he enlisted a great number of literati including Song Lian and Wang Hui. In the seventh year of the Chenghua Period of the Ming Dynasty (1471), Ningyue Prefecture changed its name to Jinhua Prefecture with the governance of eight counties, and therefore, Jinhua was named as "The Land of Eight Counties". In the Ming Dynasty, the resistance against Japanese pirates was of political importance that the Yiwu soldiers as the main force of Qi Jiguang Army fought in the front and made great feats. Later in the end of

第一章　金华　Chapter One Jinhua

Ming Dynasty and early Qing Dynasty, Zhu Dadian and Zhang Guowei died at their posts in the war against the Qing army. It was the indomitabled rebellious spirit of Wuzhou people that made the Qing Government increased the number of soldiers in Wuzhou to ensure a stable political situation. At the end of Qing Dynasty, Li Shixian, the King Shi of the Taiping Heavenly Kingdom, centered on Jinhua as the commanding center of uprising in Zhejiang, and established the grand Shiwang Residence. And it has a far-reaching historic implication.

农商并举　Agricultural and Commercial Development

明清时期，金华的经济性质与成分呈现出新的变化。早熟稻的出现使双季稻成为可能，缓解了人们对青黄不接的担忧。新的农作物开始推广，如甘蔗、番薯和玉米等，也在一定程度上缓和了饥荒。这一时期引进的佛手，日后成为本地区著名的特产。然而，随着人口的增长和频繁的自然灾害，加上一些地区广布的红壤对种植粮食作物的局限，粮食供给依然是社会发展的瓶颈。在严峻的现实面前，人们改变传统的生存策略，婺商因地制宜，发挥各自优势闯出独特生存之道。

In the Ming and Qing Dynasties, the economic nature and composition of Jinhua presented new changes, The cultivation of early rice made the cultivation of double cropping rice possible and thus lessened the worries on a temporary shortage of rice. The promotion of new crops including sugar canes, sweet potatoes and maizes relieved the famine to some extent. The Fingered Citron imported at that time became a famous local product in days to come. However, the food supplies still hindered the social development because of the increasing population, the frequent natural disasters and the red soil which limited the growth of the crops. In the face of the harsh reality, Wuzhou people changed and adjusted their living ways. The businessmen also adapted to local conditions, and made the best of these conditions to create a unique way to survive.

艺文纷呈 Literature and Art Development

明清时期,金华的文化艺术出现了繁荣纷呈的局面。东阳人何士英获明宣德皇帝赏赐,历代珍藏定武《兰亭序》石刻;兰溪人胡应麟创诗学新论,建"二酉山房"藏书四万余册;由明入清的戏剧大师李渔笔耕不辍,写《笠翁十种曲》,寓生活情趣于《闲情偶寄》;徐霞客《浙游日记》歌咏双龙胜景;浦江东皋心越精通琴刻书画,东渡日本;清末永康人胡凤丹编《金华丛书》,收录历代金华先贤之文墨。婺剧、道情迅速发展,流行于金华民间。

The culture and art of Jinhua entered a flourishing era in the Ming and Qing Dynasties. He Shiying of Dong Yang was awarded by the Emperor Xuande that he could possessed the *Preface to the Orchid Pavilion Collection* which was carved on stones. Hu Yinglin from Lanxi created a new theory of poetics and built a library called "Er You Shan Fang" with a collection of more than 40 thousand books. The dramatist Li Yu in the early Qing Dynasty kept writing *Liweng's Ten Plays* and the *Xian Qing Ou Ji*, expressing his attitude towards life enjoyment; Xu Xiake extolled the beautiful scenery of Double Dragon Cave in the *Zhejiang Travel Notes*. Donggao Xinyue who was proficient in lyre-playing, seal cutting, calligraphy and painting went to Japan. Hu Fengdan of Yongkang at the end of Qing Dynasty compiled *Jinhua Series* that contains all information about Jinhua from previous scholars' works as well as Wu Opera and Daoqing developed fast and became popular among the people of Jinhua.

六、近代时期的金华 Jinhua in Modern Times

民主先声 Democratic Pioneer

19世纪末,中国在清政府的统治和西方列强的侵略下风雨飘摇。在深重的内忧外患中,国人把目光投向西方,开始思考救国良策。清末,八婺大地上同样经历着风起云涌的变革,近代产业的兴起敲开了金华走向近代的大门。1900年,金华建立龙华会,组织反清反帝活动。光复会与龙华

第一章 金华 Chapter One Jinhua

会进行多次密切联系,并以金华为光复会起义中心。在抗日战争高潮中,金华出现很多用笔杆子战斗的革命者。陈望道翻译并出版了《共产党宣言》第一个中文全译本。一代报人邵飘萍是中国新闻理论的开拓者和奠基人,对共产主义运动做了大量报道。施复亮也是早期活动家、领导者。1925 年夏,千家驹加入中国共产党,同年,钱兆鹏、章驹、刘文铭也加入共产党,建立中共金华支部。

In the late 19th century, China was in turmoil under the rule of the Qing government and the invasion of Western powers. Facing domestic disturbances and foreign aggression, Chinese learned from the Western, seeking the ways to save the nation. In the late Qing Dynasty, the evolution befell on the Land of Eight Counties where the rising modern industry accessed Jinhua to a modern era. Founded in Jinhua in 1900, Longhua League organized anti-Qing and anti-imperialism campaigns. Guangfu League and Longhua League were associated closely, setting Jinhua as the uprising center. In the climax of the Anti-Japanese War, there appeared a lot of revolutionists who fought by writing. The first Chinese version of the *Communist Manifesto* was translated and published by Cheng Wangdao. Being a pioneer and founder of journalism theories in China, Shao Piaoping, a newspaperman largely covered the communist movement. Shi Fuliang was an activist and leader in the early times as well. In the summer of 1925, Qian Jiaju joined the Communist Party of China, so did Qian Zhaopeng, Zhang Ju and Liu Wenming, founding the Jinhua Branch of the CPC.

浙江省抗战文化中心 The Culture Center of Anti-Japanese War of Zhejiang Province

1937 年 9 月 26 日,日军在金华火车站投下第一颗炸弹。1937 年 12 月 24 日,杭州沦陷,国民党浙江省政府内迁金华,当时不到 5 万人口的金华成为全省战时中心,抗日志士云集,掀起抗战热潮。1939 年 2 月 22 日,李友邦将军在金华创建台湾义勇队和台湾少年团,以金华为中心,开展对敌政治工作、医疗救助服务、军需品及药品生产和巡回宣传演出等抗日救国活动，这是唯一一支由台湾同胞组成的在祖国大陆参加抗战的队伍，台湾义勇队旧址在金华市酒坊巷 84 号，是我国现存唯一的台湾人民抗日遗址。1939 年 4 月 2 日，周恩来以国民政府军事委员会政治部副部长身份在金华中学礼堂发表了题为《建军的重要性与社会军事化的实施》的著名抗战演讲。

On 26th, September, 1937, the first Japanese bomb was exploded at Jinhua Railway Station. On 24th, December, 1937, Hangzhou was occupied, causing the National-Party Government of Zhejiang moved to Jinhua as the center during the war. Jinhua's population was less than 50 thousand, but its patriots gathered and started the upsurge to Japan. On 22nd, February, 1939, General Li Youbang, who founded the Taiwan Army of Volunteers and the Taiwan Juvenile Group which was the only army composed by Taiwan compatriots in the Anti-Japanese War, worked on politics again Japan, medical aid services, production of military supplies and medicines as well as publicity performances in the country. The army was located at No.84, Jiufang Lane which was the only existing Taiwanese's Anti-Japanese site. On 2nd, April, 1939, Zhou Enlai, the debuty secretary of Political Department of Military Commission of the National Government, addressed a famous anti-war speech titled *The Importance of Building the Army and the Implement of Social Militarization*.

台湾义勇队初成立时队员只有几十人，大多能讲日语、写日文。他们利用这样的优势展开对敌宣传工作，翻译敌军文件、搜集情报，阵前用日语喊话，并教化日军俘虏等。台湾少年团最小的只有 9 岁，最大的也不过 12 岁。他们通过各地巡回演讲、组织文艺汇演来宣传革命和慰劳战士。

Taiwan Army of Volunteers had only dozens of members in the beginning, most of whom could speak and write in Japanese. They made full use of this advantage to carry on campaigns against the enemy, translating Japanese documents, collecting information, yelling in Japanese in the battlefield and educating war prisoners. The youngest in the cadet was only

9-year-old, the oldest was 12. They toured around to deliver speeches and give performances to publicize revolution and convey appreciation to the soldiers.

文化驿站　Cultural Courier Station

1937年末,杭州沦陷,金华一时成为东南地区的抗战中心。金华城内柴场巷15号设东南地区两个重要的文化宣传机构——浙江省文化工作委员会和东南工作委员会。是当时中共地下党组织联络站和进步文化工作者聚会的场所。1939年10月,国民政府称金华为全国五大"文化驿站"之一。《浙江潮》《东南战线》《东南日报》《浙江日报》《战时生活》《台湾先锋》都是在金华出版。其中《浙江潮》在金华酒井巷34号创刊。在创刊词《潮头语》中的"激发民族意识,发动全民抗战"揭示了《浙江潮》的任务和使命。

In the end of 1937, Hangzhou was occupied, with Jinhua becoming the only center of anti-Japanese war in the southeast. Two most important publicizing organizations were set up in No. 15 Chaichang Lane in Jinhua city, namely, Zhejiang Commission of Culture Work and Commission of Work in Southeast, which were liaison station for CPC underground and gathering place for progressive cultural workers. In October 1939, the National Government regarded Jinhua as one of the five cultural stations nationwide. The following newspapers were all published in Jinhua, namely, *Zhejiang Tide, Southeast Front, Southeast Daily, Zhejiang Daily, Life in War, Taiwan Pioneers*, among which *Zhejiang Tide* was first issued in No.34 Jiujing Lane. In the initial publication *Chaotouyu*, it wrote that "to motivate the national awareness and to encourage nation-wide resistance", which revealed the mission of *Zhejiang Tide*.

解放金华　Emancipation of Jinhua

活跃于英士大学的中共地下党组织,将民主的火种继续播撒在金华这片土地上。随着三大战役的胜利,局势从焦灼走向明朗,直到1949年5月,解放的枪声在八婺大地上打响,金华翻开了新的篇章。

Being active in Yingshi University, the underground organization of Communist Party of China (CPC) spread democratic thoughts to Jinhua. With the victory of the three main campaigns, the situation gradually became optimistic. It was the liberation of the land in May of 1949 that opened a new page of Jinhua.

英士大学在民国年间是著名国立大学,最早创建于 1928 年。1943 年 3 月,改称国立英士大学。解放战争期间,有三支中共地下党活跃于英士大学,引导学生活动。在革命思想的熏陶下,许多进步学生毕业之后转入地下党或游击队,为金华解放和全国解放贡献力量。解放战争时期活跃于金华的三支部队主要是路西金萧支队、路南第六支队和路东东磐支队,配合解放军取得了金华的解放。二野三兵团十二军三十五师渡过富春江向兰溪进军,兰溪县城是金华地区第一个解放的县城,为堵截国民党军南逃,十二军三十五师师长李德生迅速占领义乌、东阳。解放军从金华向西进军,汤溪、宣平解放。磐安是浙江省大陆最后解放的一个县。

Yingshi University, a famous national university in the Republic of China, was first established in 1928. It was renamed National Yingshi University in March, 1943. During the War of Liberation, three branches of CPC underground were active in Yingshi University leading students' activities. Under the influence of revolutionary thoughts, many progressive students joined the CPC underground or guerilla forces after graduation, contributing to the liberation of Jinhua and the whole nation. The three units that were active in Jinhua during the Liberation War included Luxi Jinhua-Xiaonan Detachment, Lunan Sixth Detachment and Ludong-Dongpan Detachment. They cooperated with the Liberation Army in liberating Jinhua. The 35th Division of 12th Corps of 3rd Legion under 2nd Field of the Liberation Army crossed over the Fuchunjiang and marched into Lanxi, the first county liberated in Jinhua area. To cut off the Kuomintang fleeing south, Li Desheng, the commander of the above division, quickly occupied Yiwu and Dongyang, which were liberated on the way to pursue the remnants of Kuomintang. The Liberation Army marched to the west from Jinhua, and then Tangxi and Xuanping were liberated. Pan'an was the last county liberated within Zhejiang.

人文荟萃 Galaxy of Talents

近代金华历经民主思想的洗礼,饱受战争的伤痛,也涌现出不少能人志士。他们用画笔、诗文书写对这片土地和人民的热爱,以踏实、严谨的治学态度开拓自然科学的研究道路,影响并改变着金华乃至全国的潮流,例如国画大师——黄宾虹、人民诗人——艾青、科学之光——严济慈、史学大家——何炳松、时代歌手——施光南等。

After the baptism of democratic thoughts and sufferings of the war, many capable people of ideals and integrity came forth in the modern Jinhua. They glorified the land and the people by their paintings and poems. Their surefooted and rigorous attitude in developing the study of natural science has influenced Jinhua and even the whole nation. For example, Huang Binhong is reputed as the Painting Master; Ai Qing, the People's Poet; Yan Jici, the Light of Science; He Bingsong, the Historiography Master; Shi Guangnan, the Singer of the Times.

第三节 金华地质地貌 Jinhua Geology and Landform

金华这片神奇的大地深处,蕴藏着各种矿产宝石。从遥远的时代起,一次次地质运动形成了金华独有的自然风貌和矿产资源。现在我们的旅游资源和工业材料都是来自远古的馈赠。金衢盆地,形成于晚燕山期。金华位于金衢盆地东部,以山地、丘陵为主。穿越盆地的江河分属三大水系:钱塘江、瓯江和椒江。金华境内的河段有武义江、东阳江、金华江和兰江等。金华江在金华盆地中间蜿蜒穿越而过,北山、南山和东边大盘山脉把金华盆地紧紧揽在怀里,这一独特的地形地貌被人们形象地称为"三面环山夹一川,盆地错落涵三江"。

In the depth of this magical land, Jinhua is rich in mineral resources and precious stones. Since the ancient times, geological movements had contributed to the unique natural scenery and mineral resources. The tourism resources and industrial materials were all bestowed by nature in the ancient times. The Jinhua-Quzhou Basin was formed in the late Yanshan Tectonic Period. Located in the east side of the basin, Jinhua is dotted with hills and mountains. The rivers flowing through the basin belong to three-river systems: Qiangtang River, Qujiang River and Jiaojiang River. The reaches within Jinhua are Wuyi River, Dongyang River, Jinhua River and Lan River etc. The Jinhua River winds through the basin, which is cuddled in the center by the North Mountain, South Mountain and the Dapan Moutain in the east. The unique landform is vividly described as "Surrounded by mountains in three sides cuddling a river, the basin is dotted with three rivers ".

金华地区位于扬子板块与东南板块之间。金华曾经是海洋，经过地质演变，直到两亿多年前才成为稳定的陆地，1亿多年前成为现在的丘陵地貌。金华盆地是我国南方著名的红色盆地之一，也是浙江省最大的中生代陆相盆地。金华盆地介于千里岗山脉、仙霞岭山脉、金华山脉、大盘山山脉之间。

Jinhua is situated between the Yangtze Plate and the Southeast Plate. Once it was an ocean, and did not become a stable continent until 200 million years ago, forming the present mountainous land until 100 million years ago after geological movements. Jinhua basin is one of the famous red basins in southern China, and the largest basin in the Mesozoic era in Zhejiang Province. The basin sits among the Qianligang Mountains, Xianxialing Mountains, Jinhua Mountains and Dapan Mountains.

地质年代的划分和研究是通过岩石和化石的历史来确定的。地质年代最大的单位称为"宙"，往下依次分为代、纪、世。它们对应的地层或地质纪录则称为"宇、界、系、统"。描述时间的时候，用"早、中、晚"。描述空间（地层顺序）的时候，就用"下、中、上"。时间再往下还可细分到期、时，对应地层称为阶、时带。

第一章 金华 Chapter One Jinhua

The classification and research of geochronology are determined by the age of rocks and fossils. The largest geological times scale is "Eon", and then subdivides into "Era", "period" and "Epoch" in turn. The corresponding layers of rock or geological events are "Eonothem, Erathem, System, Series". Geologists qualify these units as "Early, Mid and Late" when referring to time, and "Lower, Middle and Upper" when referring to the corresponding space. Time can be further divided into "Age and Ma", with the corresponding Stage and Numerical Age.

火山岩是火山熔浆冷凝而成,在侏罗纪和白垩纪时期,金华的火山运动非常频繁。磐安大盘山、兰溪金鸡岩、东阳八面山都是火山活动的遗迹。

Volcanic rock is formed from magma which cools quickly after eruption. During the Jurassic and Cretaceous periods, volcano eruptions were very frequent in Jinhua. Dapan Mountain in Pan'an, Jinji Rock in Lanxi and Bamian Mountain in Dongyang are all relics of volcano eruptions.

在金华发现有很多火山蛋,火山蛋是火山喷发时它的岩浆在空中旋转跌落到火山灰后,岩浆团形成的纺锤形或圆球形的岩石。它和恐龙蛋长得有点儿像,区别就是恐龙蛋一般都是一窝多个的,恐龙蛋有壳,剖面有蛋白蛋黄挤压的痕迹。

Many volcanic egg were found in Jinhua, which were formed when showers of magma were thrown into the air and then fell down into the ash, becoming fusiform or round rocks. They look like dinosaur eggs, but the latter are usually found in a nest, There were traces of the eggs while clashing with the yolk from the cross-section view.

丹霞地貌 Danxia Landform

晚侏罗系到早白垩系的一系列地质活动构筑了永康盆地。中生代晚期到新生代间,盆地逐渐隆升,结束了红层沉积,不断遭受侵蚀之后,最终形成了以方岩为代表的丹霞地貌群。

Yongkang basin was formed by a series of geological movements in late Jurassic and early Cretaceous system. From the late Mesozoic Era to the Cenozoic Era, the basin was uplifted gradually, ending the sedimentation of red rocks, which, after repeated erosions, finally forming the Danxia landform represented by the Nosean.

方岩地区的方山形地貌特征为"顶平、身陡、麓缓",这些山顶海拔高度大都在 380 米左右,在 8.5 万平方米范围聚集了 15 座这一类型的丹霞地貌山体。

The nosean landscape in Fangyan area is characterized by flat top, steep cliff, which is slow at the foot of the hill. There are 15 hills of similar Danxia landform within 85 thousand square meters, the top of which is about 380 metres above the sea level.

徐霞客浙游日记中有将近一半的篇幅在研究双龙洞的喀斯特地貌。双龙洞是水平发展的溶洞,简称为平洞,以流水沉积为主。

Xu Xiake had written half of the whole words to describe the Karst landform of Double Dragon Cave in his *Zhejiang Travel Note*. Double Dragon Cave develops horizontally, which is called horizontal cave briefly , formed by sedimentation of flowing water.

里面有很多石钟乳、石笋、石柱,这是含有碳酸钙的水滴从洞顶裂隙中渗出,不断向下滴落,在洞顶结晶形成石钟乳,在洞底沉积则形成石笋。两者不断生长,最后连为一体则成为石柱。这些石钟乳、石笋和石柱大约发育于晚更新系末期(距今 3 万年左右)。

There are lots of stalactites, stalagmites and stone columns inside. The water loaded with calcium carbonate from the factures of the cave dripped down continuously, which was crystallized on the roof (stalactite), and deposited at the bottom (stalagmite). These two kept on growing until they grew into a whole piece, becoming stone columns. These stalactites, stalagmites and stone columns were formed approximately in the late Pleistocene (about 30 thousand years ago).

8 亿年前,金华地区西北部是滨海地带,东南部是岛屿、陆地。晚泥盆纪起至早二叠纪止,在兰溪等滨海沼泽区,蕨类植物得到了发展。

800 million years ago, the northwest of Jinhua was the littoral belt. The southeast part was islands or lands. From the late Devonian to the early Permian, ferns spread to the littoral marshes in Lanxi.

1.5 亿年前的侏罗纪,金华地区的造山运动剧烈。一些松树、柏树、樟树被埋入地下,经历一系列化学作用之后,形成硅化石。

During the Jurassic period, 150 million years ago mountain building move ment was intense in Jinhua area. Some pine trees, cypress trees and camphor trees were buried underground, which became silicified wood after a series of chemical processes.

在白垩纪时期,金华地区出现不少河流,河域中生活着很多鱼类、螺类等生物。这是金华鱼类、螺类的化石,狼鳍鱼化石一般体长在 10 厘米左右,生活于淡水中。

During the Cretaceous period, a number of rivers appeared in Jinhua area, which accomodated a variety of fishes and snails. These are the fossils of the above-mentioned fish and snail. The fossil of Lycoptera, was about 10 cm in length, lived in fresh water.

鸭嘴龙　Hadrosaur

到距今 7000 万年前的白垩纪晚期,金华地区尤其是东阳、永康一带生活着恐龙。金衢盆地是浙江省最大的白垩世盆地,尤其在东阳发现了完整的东阳龙、还挖掘出鸭嘴龙类骨化石。

In the late Cretaceous period about 70 million years ago, dinosaurs lived in Jinhua area, particularly in Dongyang and Yongkang. The Jinhua-Quzhen Basin is the largest Cretaceous basin in Zhejiang Province. The fossil of a complete Dongyang dragon and other fossils like hadrosaur have been unearthed in Dongyang.

鸭嘴龙体长一般为 7～15 米,属鸟臀类恐龙。鸭嘴龙是有名的 "多齿",它嘴里上下左右都有并列的几排牙齿,每个牙床上最多可以长 500 多个牙齿,所以总共的牙齿最多可达 2000 多个。

Hadrosaur was about 7-15 metres long, belonging to the ornithischian. Hadrosaur was a famous dinosaur with rows of teeth. There were more than 500 teeth on each teeth ridge, totaling 2000 altogether at the most.

2007 年 9 月,浙江东阳发现了大型的巨龙类恐龙化石,古生物专家确定为新属新种。这是一种生活在中生代晚白垩世早期的大型蜥脚类巨龙,命名为 "中国东阳龙"。挖掘出来的东阳龙身长 15.6 米,高约 5 米。

In September 2007, the fossil of the giant Titanosauria was found in Dongyang Zhejiang, which was classified as a new genus and a new species by paleontologists. It was a type of Titanosauriformes called Dongyang dragon of China, which lived in the late Mesozoic Era and the early Cretaceous period. The unearthed Dongyang dragon is about 15.6 m long and 5 m tall.

1972 年,浙江省博物馆在汤溪境内采集到一个破碎的右胫骨和一个保存较为完好的后足。该标本经中科院专家鉴定,定名为吉蓝泰龙属的新种 "浙江吉蓝泰龙"。这只吉蓝泰龙据估计体长可达 8 米左右,属肉食性恐龙。

In 1972, Zhejiang Provincial Museum found a cracked right tibia and a well-preserved metapodium in Tangxi. According to experts of the Chinese Academy of Sciences, the specimen was named "Chilantaisaurus of Zhejiang" as a new species of the genus of Chilantaisaurus. Which is about 8 metres long and carnivorous.

金华北山双龙洞出土了脊椎动物化石 48 种,包括 1 种爬行类和 47 种哺乳类。它们生活在大约 8000 年前,当时的气温比现在高 4 摄氏度,属亚热带湿热性气候。

48 types of vertebrates fossils were excavated in the Double Dragon Cave of the North Mountain in Jinhua, including a sort of reptile and 47 types of mammals. They lived about 8 thousand years ago, with the temperature 4 degrees higher than that of the present, belonging to the humid subtropical climate.

第一章 金华 Chapter One Jinhua

双龙洞全新世动物群中有 5 种已经灭绝。距今 5000 年的一次降温事件以及后来的人类活动可能是它们灭绝的直接原因。另外 16 种动物，则为适应变冷的气候向南迁移，如今依然生活在更南的地域，如海南、东南亚等热带地区。

Five types of animals were already extinct among the Holocene faunas in Double Dragon Cave. The sharp drop of temperature about 5 thousand years ago and the subsequent human activities probably led to extinction of these animals. The other 16 types of animals migrated to the south to accommodate the cold weather, which still exist in the warmer southern regions, such as Hainan, tropical areas of Southeast Asia.

金华境内发现的矿产有 56 余种，可供开发利用的有 32 种。金华的矿石分为金属矿和非金属矿。金属矿主要有金、银等贵金属矿以及钼、锡等。银矿的化学性质稳定，除了可用于制作各类工艺品外，还用于牙齿修复、工业等方面。金华地区共发现银矿产地 4 处，储量 118 吨。武义垄坑银矿是明代时期的银矿，产量巨大，每年交银税高达 800～2331 两，后因矿工起义停采。

More than 56 kinds of minerals have been discovered in Jinhua, with 32 of them worthwhile for exploitation. The ores in Jinhua include metal and nonmetal ores. Metal ores of Jinhua are mainly precious metals like gold and silver as well as molybdenum and tin. Silver's chemical property is stable. It can be used to make handworks and repair teeth, or applied in industry. Four mines have been prospected with silver ores, with a reserve of 118 tons. Longkeng silver mine of Wuyi was extracted with huge output in Ming Dynasty, whose annual revenue mounted to 800～2331 *liang*. Later on the mine was shut down because of the strike of miners.

金华的非金属矿主要有萤石矿、石灰岩、花岗岩等，多是用于工业的材料。萤石又称氟石，是火山岩浆冷却时分离出的含氟溶液，在沿裂隙上升过程中与钙离子结合而成，因在紫外光下发出强烈荧光得名。河姆渡人在 7000 年以前已经用萤石作装饰品了。武义的萤石矿是亚洲第一大矿,藏量达 350 万吨。萤石业内有个说法:"中国萤石看浙江,浙江萤石看金华,金华萤石看武义。"剧烈的火山运动除了带来丰富的矿产之外,还给武义带来了地热温泉。目前,武义县被自然资源部命名为"中国温泉之城"。

There are various nonmetal ores in Jinhua, mainly including fluorite ore, limestone, granite etc, most of which are materials applied in industry. Fluorite, also called fluorspar, is formed from fluorine-laden solution when volcanic magma cooled down. When rising upward along the cracks, it combined with calcium ion, which let off bright fluorescent light under the ultraviolet light, thus getting the name Fluorite. Hemudu people had used fluorite for decoration 7000 years ago. Wuyi boasts the largest fluorite mine in Asia, with a reserve of 3.5 million tons. There is a saying in the fluorite industry: "Looking for fluorite in China. Go to Zhejiang. Looking for fluorite in Zhejiang. Go to Jinhua. Looking for fluorite in Jinhua. Go to Wuyi". Apart from the abundant mineral ores, violent volcano movements bring geothermal energy and hot spring for Wuyi as well. At present, Wuyi county is named as "Hot Spring City of China" by the Ministry of Land and Resources.

第四节　金华行政区域
Jinhua Administrative Divisions

省辖地级市金华下辖 9 个县级行政区域,包括 2 个市辖区,4 个县级市和 3 个县。

The provincial prefecture-level city Jinhua administers 9 county-level divisions, including 2 districts, 4 county-level cities and 3 counties.

一、婺城区[②]　Wucheng District

婺城区地处浙江省中西部、金衢盆地腹部,东邻金东区,南毗武义县,西和西南毗连龙游县和遂昌市,北接兰溪市,是中国优秀旅游城市、

第一章 金华 Chapter One Jinhua

国家历史文化名城、中国十佳宜游城市、国家园林城市金华市的核心区。总面积 1391.24 平方千米,总人口 62.73 万人,全区共有 30 个少数民族,其中畲族为世居少数民族。

Located at the mid-west part of Zhejiang Province and the center of Jinhua – Quzhou Basin, Wucheng District borders Jindong District in the east, Wuyi County in the south, Longyou County in the west, Suichang City in the southwest and Lanxi City in the north. Wucheng District is the core area of Jinhua City which is the Excellent City for Traveling in China, the National Historical and Cultural City, China Top-Ten tourism City and the National Garden City. Covering a total area of 1391.24 square kilometers, Wucheng District has a population of 627,300, with 30 minorities, and She is the local minority.

婺城历史悠久,是人文荟萃的吴越古城。东汉初平三年（192 年）设长山县,后为东阳郡,陈天嘉三年（565 年）后改东阳郡为金华郡,始有金华之名。隋文帝开皇十三年（593 年）废郡置州,以其地于天文为婺女分野,故名婺州。婺城素有"江南小邹鲁"之称,在 1800 多年的建城史中,创造了灿烂的文化。有国内尚存最早城墙之一的唐宋子城遗迹、李清照吟诵千古绝唱的八咏楼等。

As a gathering place of humanities, Wucheng is an ancient city in Wu and Yue period. Jinhua began its name in 565 AD, when Dongyang County, which was established in 192 AD, changed its name into Jinhua County. In 593 AD, Jinhua was named Wuzhou. Wucheng is famous for the name of "Small Zoulu of the southern China" , for its gorgeous culture created within a history of more than 1800 years. Jinhua owns the most ancient city wall existing in China—relics in the Tang and Song Dynasties, Bayong Building that Li Qingzhao delivered her unprecedented poem for.

婺城属亚热带季风气候,四季分明,气温适中,素为江南鱼米之乡,非常适合居住和旅游。婺城北有国家 4A 级旅游景区双龙国家级风景名胜区,南有"金华桂花谷"城郊湖山型仙源湖省级旅游度假区。近年来,乡村旅游发展势头良好,全国环境优美乡莘畈乡、"中国美丽田园"梯田景观前十强塔石高山梯田等特色乡村旅游点星罗棋布,目前全区拥有省特色旅游村（点）8个。

Thanks to its subtropical climate, Wucheng has a very distinctive seasons with mild temperature, Wucheng is also known as "Land of Fish and Rice in Southern China". It is suitable for people to live and travel.The national scenic spot of the Double-dragon Cave gleams in the north while the provincial tourism resort--Xianyuan Lake glistens in the south. In recent years, the countryside tourism has been developing rapidly with scenic spots scattering over the place such as Xinfan County which is one of the top-ten terrace landscapes in Chinese beautiful countryside. Till now, there are eight typical provincial tourism villages.

婺城繁花似锦,是名满江南的大美花都。婺城是著名的中国茶花之乡、中国桂花之乡、中国苗木（盆景）之乡,从 2009 年起,婺城区依托丰富的花卉产业资源,连续举办了多届中国仙源湖桂花节、婺城茶花节、婺城油菜花节,营造"山花烂漫•美丽婺城"形象,并举办了多个节庆活动,着力打造"仙山胜水•浙中花都"特色旅游品牌。

Wucheng District where flowers bloom is renowned as City of Flowers. It is the Land of Camellia, the Land of Osmanthus and the Land of Nursery Plants in China. In 2009, relying on the flower industry, there held many festivals and conferences such as China • Xianyuan Lake Osmanthus Festival, Wucheng Camellia Festival, Wucheng Brassica Campestris Festival to shape an image of "a Charming Wucheng with Blooming Flowers", as well as many events of entertainment to build a brand of "Fairy Mountains and Rivers in the Flowery City "at the center of Zhejiang.

二、金东区③ Jindong District

金东区成立于 2001 年 2 月,现辖 8 镇 1 乡 2 街道,总面积 661.8 平方千米,人口 30.5 万,地处浙江中部的金衢盆地,东邻国际小商品城——义乌,南连中国五金城永康,西接金华城区,是浙中城市群的重要核心区,也是金义黄金主轴的重要节点。全区交通便利,浙赣铁路复线、金温铁路、330 国道、03 省道贯穿全境,杭金衢高速、金丽温高速、甬金高速公路在区内均设有互通口,是金华主城区发展建设的核心板块,更是金华城市发展中最年轻的"活力新区、魅力新城"。

The Jindong District established in February 2001 has jurisdiction over 8 towns, 1 village and 2 sub-districts. The area with a population of 305,000 covers 661.8 square kilometers. It is located in Jinhua – Quzhou Basin basin of the middle part of Zhejiang, close to the international small commodity city – Yiwu in the east, connecting the Chinese hardware city Yongkang in the south and Jinhua urban area in the west. It is a substantially important in the city agglomeration of the mid Zhejiang and of the Jinhua-Yiwu golden axis. The transportation of the district is convenient, the Zhejiang-Jiangxi railway alternative line, the Jinhua-Wenzhou railway, the 330 national highway and the 03 provincial highway run through the whole district. Meanwhile, HangJinqu Expressway, JinLiwen Expressway and Yongjin Expressway are equipped with interflows. It is the core place of development and construction of the main urban area of Jinhua, and also the youngest "New Energetic District and New Glamourous District" in the area.

路网发达、交通便利。杭长高铁等 3 条铁路、4 条省级以上高速贯穿全境,高铁至杭州 40 分钟,至上海约 90 分钟,至义乌机场半小时,至杭州萧山机场 1 小时。

Three high-speed railways such as Hangzhou-Changsha line and four provincial expressways speed through the whole territory. Through high-speed rail way, It takes 40 minutes to Hangzhou, 90 minutes to Shanghai, 30 minutes to Yiwu and 1 hour to Hangzhou Xiaoshan Airport.

名人荟萃、人杰地灵。金东文化底蕴深厚,是一代文宗宋濂、新民主主义革命先驱施复亮、人民音乐家施光南、诗坛泰斗艾青、史学家吴晗等才俊的故乡。

Jindong District is full of profound culture producing a galaxy of talents and intellectuals such as Song Lian-the well-known literary master, Shi Fuliang-the pioneer of new democratic revolution, Shi Guangnan-the people's musician, Ai Qing-the best poet in poetry and the historian Wu Han.

配套完善、产业集聚。建有浙中首个双线接入的国家 A 类互联网数据中心和中国华东云计算中心,拥有浙中西部唯一的"无水港"和公共型保税仓库,农产品、汽配、建材、苗木等六大专业市场。

With industrial agglomeration and perfect supporting facilities, the Jindong district has established the first national A level Internet data center and the East China cloud computing center. At the west of the central Zhejiang, it is unique in six professional markets including "waterless port", public bonded warehouse, agricultural products, automobile accessories, building materials and nursery stock.

环境优美、宜游宜居。地处中国十佳宜居城市、中国优秀旅游城市、国家级历史文化名城之中,区内宗教、古建、文化和乡村休闲等优良级资源达 70 余个。

With beautiful surroundings and reputation for tourism as well as for living, Jindong District is renowned as one of the top ten livable cities of China, Chinese excellent tourist city, one of state-list historical and cultural cities. There are over 70 excellent religious, historically architectural, cultural, rural and leisure resorts in the district.

三、东阳④ Dongyang

东阳地处浙江省中部,全市总面积 1739 平方千米,辖有 6 个街道、11 个镇和 1 个乡,总人口 80.2 万。

Dongyang lies in the central area of Zhejiang Province, covering an area of 1739 square kilometers. It administrates 6 streets, 11 villages and 1 town, with a population totalling 802 000.

东阳地形以丘陵和盆地为主,东阳江、东阳南江横贯全境。东阳属亚热带季风气候区，气候温和，雨量充沛，四季分明，日平均气温 17.1℃，年平均日照 2002 小时，年平均降雨量 1351 毫米。

The landform mainly consists of hills and basins. Dongyang River and Dongyan Nanjiang River traverse the city. It is situated in the subtropical monsoon climate zone with mild weather, rich rainfall and a clear seasonal distinction. The daily temperature averages 17.1℃, the annual sun exposure averages 2,002 hours and the annual rainfall averages 1351 millimeters.

东阳历史悠久，东汉兴平二年（公元 195 年）建县，迄今已有 1800 多年的历史。1988 年，经国务院批准，东阳撤县设市。东阳人文荟萃，英才辈出，如唐代冯宿、舒元舆，南宋乔行简，明末张国维等，近现代有北伐名将金佛庄、新闻先驱邵飘萍等。

Dongyang with a long history was first set up in the second year of XingPing Reign of the East Han Dynasty (195 A.D.), and it has been over 1800 years so far. In 1988, it was ratified by the State Council to be a city from a county. Dongyang has a galaxy of celebrities—Feng Su and Shu Yuanyu of the Tang Dynasty, Qiao Xingjian of the Southern Song Dynasty, Zhang Guowei in the late Ming Dynasty. Jin Fozhuang, a famous general of northern expedition and Shao Piaoping, an outstanding journalist in modern times.

东阳是著名的"教育之乡"。东阳自古以来就有"兴学重教、勤耕苦读"的传统，朱熹、吕祖谦、陆游等曾到东阳"石洞书院"讲学传道，明代开国文臣宋濂所撰写的《送东阳马生序》，数百年来脍炙人口。历史上，东阳进士题名共有 305 人。据统计，到 2007 年底，在国内外具有高级职称的东阳籍人士达 8000 多人，博士和博士后 800 余人，东阳籍院士 10 人。

Dongyang as a Land of Education has the tradition of promoting education and diligent farming and learning. The renowned scholars such as Zhu Xi, Lv Zuqian and Lu You went to Shi Dong Academy to deliver lectures, Song Lian, the civilian court official among founders of the Ming Dynasty, wrote the national famous *Farewell Words to Mr. Ma of Dongyang*.

There were 305 *jinshi* in Dongyang in the history of China. At the end of 2007, it was recorded that there were more than 8000 Dongyang talents with senior titles including more than 800 doctors and post-doctors, and 10 Dongyang academicians.

东阳还享有建筑之乡、百工之乡、恐龙之乡等美誉。改革开放以来，东阳经济社会持续快速发展，是浙江省首批小康县市、首批文明城市、首批旅游经济强市等。

Dongyang also enjoys a good reputation of Land of Architecture, Craftsmanship, Dinosaurs. Since the reform and opening-up policy, Dongyang has kept a rapid and stable development, and has attained outstanding titles such as the First Well-off Counties, Civilized Cities, Powerful Tourist-Economy City.

四、兰溪⑤ Introduction of Lanxi

兰溪市位于浙江省中西部，地处钱塘江中游，金衢盆地北缘，地理坐标为北纬 29°1'20"～29°27'30"，东经 119°13'30"～119°53'50"，东西长 67.5 千米，南北宽 38.5 千米，距金华市区 20.5 千米，杭州 132 千米，总面积 1 313 平方千米，2013 年末户籍总人口 66.67 万人。

Lanxi is located in the mid-west of Zhejiang Province, in the midstream of Qiantang River and at the northern margin of the Jinhua-Quzhou Basin. It is at 29°1'20" to 29°27'30" N and 119°13'30" to 119°53'50" E. It is 67.5 km from the east to the west and 38.5 km from the south to the north. It is about 20.5 km to Jinhua downtown, 132 km to Hangzhou, with a total area of 1,313 square km and with a total registered population of 666,700 at the end of 2013.

兰溪市内水系属钱塘江水系，主要有三江（衢江、金华江、兰江）五溪（梅溪、甘溪、赤溪、游埠溪、马达溪）组成。市树市花分别为樟树和兰花。

Its water system belongs to Qiantang River, covering three rivers (Qujiang River, Jinhua River, Lan River) and five streams (Meixi, Ganxi,

Chixi, Youbu and Mada). Camphor tree and orchid is City Tree and Flower respectively.

兰溪市属亚热带季风气候,温暖湿润,四季分明,雨量适中,无霜期长,夏季高温,冬春寒潮,全年平均气温 17.7 ℃,冬季平均 5.4 ℃,历史最低温度 -8.2 ℃,夏季平均 29.8 ℃,历史最高 41.3 ℃,年平均降水量 1439 mm,无霜期平均 265 天。

Lanxi is situated in the subtropical monsoon climate area which is warm and moist, with clear distinction seasons, adequate rainfall and long frost-free period. It is hot in summer, cold in winter and wet in spring. The average annual temperature is around 17.7 ℃. The average temperature in winter is 5.4 ℃ , with the lowest being -8.2 ℃ , and 29.8 ℃ in summer with the highest being 41.3 ℃ in history. The annual average rainfall is 1439mm and the annual frost-free period averages about 265 days.

兰溪山灵水秀,风光旖旎,既具文物古董,又多风景名胜,旅游资源十分丰富。兰溪是黄大仙故里,诸葛八卦村被誉为"世界旅游极品",六洞山、白露山、兰荫山被载入《中国名胜大字典》,当代名媛赵四小姐故里的"地下长河"为全国洞府泉流航游之冠。兰溪名人辈出,五代高僧贯休、宋代名儒金履祥、明代文字家胡应麟、清代戏剧大师李渔、现代文字家曹聚仁、当代世界摄影大师郎静山等名噪海内外。

Lanxi is rich in tourist resources, not only with grand mountains and graceful rivers but also with cultural relics and natural landscapes. It is the home of Huang Daxian. The Zhuge Eight-Diagrams village in Lanxi is renowned as the "Excellence of World Tourism" , Liudong Mountain, Bailu Mountain and Lanyin Mountain are listed in *Dictionary of Chinese Places of Interests*. The Underground River, which is the home village of Ms. Zhaosi, the lady of quality, tops all the places of the type in China. The galaxy of celebrities including the senior monk Guanxiu of the Five Dynasties, the famous general Jin Lvxiang of the Song Dynasty, the writer Hu Yinglin of the Ming Dynasty the drama master Li Yu of the Qing Dynasty, the modern litterateur Cao Juren, the modern photographer Lang Jingshan—are world-famous.

五、磐安　Introduction of Pan'an

磐安是一个隶属于中国浙江省金华市的山城，以其清新的空气和美丽的风景而闻名，这使得它成为新兴的旅游区，接待周边城市的游客。总面积 1196 平方千米，20.9 万人口，辖 19 个乡镇。磐安县在抗战烽火中的1939 年设县。1958 年，全境并入东阳。1983 年，恢复磐安县。

Pan'an County is a mountainous county within the Jinhua territory of Zhejiang Province, and is known for fresh air and beautiful scenery. This makes it a growing tourist area for people of nearby cities. With a total area of 1196 square kilometers, it has a population of 209 thousand and over 19 subdivisions are under its jurisdiction. Pan'an county was established in 1939 during the war of resistance against Japan. In 1958, it was incorporated into Dongyang County，and in 1983, restored.

磐安旅游资源丰富，是江南最大的孔氏聚居地，拥有玉山古茶场和榉溪孔氏家庙两家"全国重点文物保护单位"和全国唯一药用植物国家自然保护区——大盘山自然保护区，国家 4A 级景区的百丈潭和夹溪十八涡等。磐安素有"群山之祖，诸水之源"之称，是钱塘江、瓯江、灵江和曹娥江四大水系的主要发源地。磐安又被誉为"天然氧吧"。全县森林覆盖率 75.4 %。

Pan'an County is rich in tourism resources and is the largest Kong offsprings in the south of the Yangtze River. Two national key cultural relic units (Yushan tea plantation relic and Kongshi Family of Juxi) and one national medicinal plant protection area (Dapanshan National Nature Reserve) are right here. It is also nation-widely known by 4A tourism resorts, such as Baizhang Pond and Jiaxi Scenic Resort. Pan'an county is known as "the Father of Mountains and Waters"，and is the birthplace of four major river systems: Qiantang River, Oujiang, Lingjiang River and Caoe River. It is also called "the Natural Oxygen Bar" , since the county's percentage of forest coverage is up to 75.4 %.

磐安钟灵毓秀、人杰地灵。自唐会昌以来，有武状元1人，武进士6人，文进士70人。萧统曾隐居大盘山，潜心编撰《文选》。陆游在磐安留下了"山重水复疑无路，柳暗花明又一村"的千古绝唱。

Pan'an County is a place endowed with fine spirits and a place propitious for great men. Since the Tang Dynasty, there was one scholar of martial arts, 6 *jinshi* of martial arts and 70 *jinshi* of literature. Xiao Tong lived in seclusion in Dapanshan and concentrated on compiling the *Literature Selection*. Lu You wrote "Where hills bend, streams wind and the pathway seems to end/ past dark willows and flowers in bloom lies another village" in pan'an, which has been an eternal masterpiece.

六、浦江　Introduction of Pujiang

浦江县位于浙江中部，金华市北部，东南接义乌市，西南与兰溪市毗连，西北和建德接壤，距金华城区46千米。截至2013年，浦江县面积920平方千米，辖7镇5乡3街道、409个行政村和20个社区，户籍人口38万。

Pujiang County is located in the center of Zhejiang Province, in the north of Jinhua, bordered by Yiwu and Lanxi in the southeast and Southwest, Jiande in the northwest, and is 46 km to the downtown of Jinhua. It exercises jurisdiction over seven towns, five townships, three residential districts, twenty neighborhood communities and 409 villages with a population of 380,000, covering an area of 920 km^2 by the end of 2013 .

浦江山清水秀，享有"休闲胜地"之称。县内旅游资源丰富，比如4A级景区仙华山以及最近开发的白石湾景区、宝掌幽谷、神丽峡、通济湖和江南第一家。江南第一家为郑氏家族，在浦江生活了十五世。浦江上山文化遗址是迄今为止发现的最早的新时期文化遗址，是浙江文化历史上的一颗璀璨的明珠。

It enjoys splendid and beautiful mountains and rivers with called name of "Center for Relaxation." It is rich in ecological tourism resources with the AAAA level tourist area of Xianhua Mountain and other recentlly developed scenic spots such as Baishiwan, Baozhang Valley, Shenli Gorge, Tongji Lake and The First Family of Southern China. The Zheng Family Clan descendants have been living in Pujiang for fifteen generations. It also has "Shangshan Cultural Relics," which has been the earliest site of New Stone Age discovered so far in the bright pearl history of Zhejiang culture.

浦江历史悠久,东汉兴平二年（195 年）建县,唐天宝十三年（754 年）置浦阳县,五代吴越天宝三年（910 年）改浦阳为浦江,沿用至今。浦江人杰地灵,名人辈出,比如明朝开国文臣宋濂,日本篆刻之父东皋心越等。浦江也被誉为"中国书画之乡""中国民间艺术之乡"等。浦江工业多样化,其中水晶和五金制锁占据了市场的 70 %,成为中国水晶和制锁的集散中心。因此,浦江也被誉为"水晶之都"和"制锁之城"。

It was set up as a county in the second year of Donghan Xingping (195 A.D.) and named Pujiang County in the thirteenth year of Tianbao 745A. D. in the Tang Dynasty. The name was changed to Pujiang County in the third year of Wuyue Tianhao (910 A.D.), which is still in use today. There is no lack of talented people. Among them, the most famous are Song Lian known as the founding minister of the Ming Dynatsy and Donggao Xinyue who went to Japan and was known as the father of seal cutting there. Pujiang is also named as "County of Chinese Painting and Calligraphy" and "County of Chinese Folk Art", etc. The industry in Pujiang is varied, among which crystals and padlocks take up to 70 % market sale, which makes Pujiang the collecting and distributing center of crystal and padlocks in China. Thus it is named "Crystal Capital" and "Padlock Center".

七、武义[6] Wuyi

武义县隶属浙江省金华市。位于浙江省中部,介于北纬 28°31'～29°03', 东经 119°27'～119°58'。武义县面积 1577 平方千米,辖 3

个街道、15 个乡镇。武义县境属中亚热带季风气候,四季分明,温和湿润,雨量丰沛。自 1962 年至 2005 年的 44 年间,年平均温度 17.07 ℃,无霜期平均在 242 天左右,年平均降水量 1 474.49 毫米,年平均相对湿度 80.09 %,年平均日照时数为 1891.51 小时,年均风速 1.33 米 / 秒,常年多东北风。

Wuyi county of Jinhua is located at 28° 32"~29° 41' N and 119° 14"~120° 46' E in the middle of Zhejiang. It covers an area of 1577 square kilometers, governing three sub-districts and 15 towns. Wuyi is situated in the subtropical monsoon climate area with distinctive seasons, warm and moist climate and abundant rainfall. During 44 years from 1962 to 2005, the annual temperature averages 17.07 ℃ , the frost-free period averages 242 days, the averages annual rainfall is 1474.49 millimeters, the averages annual relative humidity is 80.09%, the averages annual sunshine is 1891.51 hours and the averages annual wind speed is 1.33m/s.

唐天授二年(公元 691 年),永康西境始置武义县,隶婺州。传武则天执政时,新设郡县均冠以 "武" 字,因县东有百义山,故以武义为名县。

In the second year of Tianshou Period of the Tang Dynasty (691A.D.), Wuyi County was established within west Yongkang, belonging to Wuzhou. It is said that the character of Wu was used to name each newly-set county or prefecture because of Wu Zetian who was then in power, moreover, there was a Baiyi Mountain at the east side, so the name of Wuyi came into being.

武义山川秀美,物华天宝。萤石储量居全国之首,温泉资源 "华东第一、全国一流",素有 "萤石之乡、温泉之城" 的美誉。萤石蕴藏量约 4000 万吨,量大质优。溪里温泉日出水量超 2 500 吨,水温 42.6~44 ℃,含多种对人体有益微量元素。尚有矿泉水、金、银、钴、硫等矿藏。武义 "宣莲" 是中国三大名莲之一。有机茶颁证面积和产量居全国之冠,是 "中国有机茶之乡"。

Wuyi with grand mountains is rich in resources. In particular, the fluorite reserves rank No.1 in China. The hot spring is awarded with the title of No.1 in east China and the whole country. Wuyi is the homeland of fluorite and hot spring. There are about 40 million tons of fluorite with good quality. The daily hot spring from rivers is more than 2500 tons with water temperature of 42.6～44 ℃. The hot spring contains a large number of trace elements which are beneficial to human. There are also mineral resources such as mineral water, gold, silver, diamond and sulphur. Xuanlian of Wuyi is one of the three famous lotuses in China. The approved area of organic tea ranks the first in the whole country, and thus, Wuyi is renowned as the Land of China's Organic Tea.

武义是新文化运动先驱,湖畔诗人潘漠华,著名经济学家千家驹,著名工笔画大师潘洁兹的故乡。武义景观丰富,有俞源太极星象古建筑群、熟溪桥、上甘塔红军标语、吕祖谦墓和明招寺等省重点文物保护单位。有省级龙潭—郭洞风景名胜区。华山、台山、石鹅岩、清风寨、寿仙谷等市、县级风景区。

Wuyi is the hometown of the new-culture-movement pioneer and lake poet Pan Mohua, the famous economist Qian Jiaju and the well-known Gongbi-painting master Pan Jiezi. What's more, Wuyi is rich in historical and natural landscapes. For historical ones, the ancient buildings of taichi Star of Yuyuan Village, and many provincial cultural-relic protection officials such as Shuxi Bridge, Shangganta slogans of the Red Army, Tomb of Lv Zuqian and Mingzhao Temple. For natural ones, there is the provincial-level Longtan-Guodong Scenic Spot, and city-level or county-level scenic spots such as Hua Mountain, Tai Mountain, Shi'e Rock, Qingfengzhai and Shouxiangu,etc.

八、义乌⑦ Introduction of Yiwu

义乌位于金衢盆地东部,东经119°49′至120°17′,北纬29°02′13″至29°33′40″,地处浙江省地理中心。东邻东阳,南界永康、武义,西连金华、兰溪,北接诸暨、浦江。至省会杭州百余千米。

Yiwu is located in the east of the Jinhua-Quzhou Basin and the geographical center of Zhejiang Province, at 119°49' - 120°17' E and 29° 02'13" - 29°33'40" N. Yiwu adjoins Dongyang in the east, Yongkang and Wuyi in the south, Jinhua and Lanxi in the west, and Zhuji Pujiang in the north, more than a hundred kilometers away from Hangzhou, the capital city of Zhejiang Province.

市境东、南、北三面群山环抱，南北长 58.15 千米，东西宽 44.41 千米，境内有中低山、丘陵、岗地、平原，土壤类型多样，光热资源丰富。义乌属亚热带季风气候，温和湿润，四季分明。年平均气温在 17℃ 左右，平均气温以七月份最高，为 29.3 ℃，一月份最低，为 4.2 ℃。年平均无霜期为 243 天左右。年平均降水量为 1100～1600 毫米之间。

The city is embraced by mountains in the south, east and north, with a distance of 58.15 km from the south to the north and 44.41 km from the east to the west. The landform and the soil types of the city are varied, including medium and low mountains, hills, hillocks and plains, and the city is rich in sunlight and heat resources. Yiwu is situated in the subtropical monsoon climate area with warm and moist climate and distinctive seasons. The average annual temperature is around 17℃, with the highest being 29.3 ℃ in July and the lowest 4.2 ℃ in January. The annual frost-free period averages about 243 days and the annual rainfall averages between 1100 to 1600 millimeters.

义乌历史悠久，建县（古称乌伤县）于公元前 222 年，并于公元 624 年，更名为义乌县，1988 年，撤县建市。义乌名人辈出，先后涌现"初唐四杰"之一骆宾王、宋代名将宗泽、金元四大名医之一朱丹溪及现代教育家陈望道、文艺理论家冯雪峰、历史学家吴晗等历史名人。

Yiwu boasts a long history, which was formed as Wushang County is 222 B.C. , renamed as Yiwu County in 624 A.D. and established as Yiwu City in 1988. It is renowned as a land of culture, and a number of celebrities were born in Yiwu, among who are Luo Bingwang, one of the four famous litterateurs in early Tang Dynasty, Zong Ze, a well-famed general of Song

Dynasty, Zhu Danxi, one of the four distinguished medical doctors of Jin and Yuan Dynasties, Chen Wangdao, contemporary educator, Feng Xuefeng, literature and art theorist, and Wu Han, historian in modern times.

义乌是中国首个也是唯一一个在县级市的国家级综合改革试点,先后被授予中国国家卫生城市、国家环保模范城市、中国优秀旅游城市、国家园林城市、国家森林城市和浙江省文明示范市等荣誉称号。

Yiwu is the first and only county-level city undertaking the national comprehensive trial reform.It was titled as the "National Health City", "National Model City for Environmental Protection", "China Top Tourist City", "National Garden City", "National Forest City" and "Zhejiang Model City for Civilization".

义乌四大家 Historic Celebrities of Yiwu-Four Masters

佛学大家——傅大士,与达摩、志公共称梁代三大士,曾为梁武帝讲经,为当时佛教界领袖,首创转轮藏以藏佛经,在佛学上多有建树,是中国文化史上的一位思想家。

Master in Buddhism: As the leader in the Buddhist circle in the Liang Dynasty, Fu Dashi once explained the lections for Liangwu Emperor. Fu Dashi, Damo (Bodhidharma) and Zhigong were called "Three Dashis" in the Liang Dynasty. Apart from inventing the revolvable closet for collecting Buddhist books, Fu Dashi made great achievements in the study of Buddhism and is an ideologist in China's cultural history.

文学大家——骆宾王(619-约687),7岁咏《鹅》,才名远播;"帝京"长篇,誉为绝唱;讨武传檄,轰动朝野;初唐四杰,名留千古。

Master in Literature: Luo Binwang (619-around 687) made his name through the poem called *Ode to Goose* composed at the age of seven. His long seven-word poem *Dijing* is regarded as a literary masterpiece and his *Official Denunciation of Empress Wu Zetian* shocked the whole society royal court at that time. As one of the four famous litterateurs in the early Tang Dynasty, Luo Binwang is well known from generation to generation.

兵学大家——宗泽 (1060—1128)，是北宋、南宋之交在抗金斗争中涌现出来的杰出政治家、军事家，文韬武略，堪称一代名将，是我国历史上著名的民族英雄。

Master in Military Strategies: Zong Ze (1060—1128), a prominent politician and military strategist in the fight against the Jin invaders in the turning period from the Northern Song Dynasty to the Southern Song Dynasty, is a famous general and national hero in Chinese history with exceptional talents in both literature and military strategies.

医学大家——朱丹溪 (1281−1358)，少年勤学，后从医学，救死扶伤，医德高尚；"阳常有余，阴常不足""相火"之论，学说远播；医学传人，历代不绝，誉为金元四大医家之一。

Master in Medicine: Zhu Danxi (1281−1358) studied hard when he was young and engaged in medical field when he grew up. With noble medical ethics he was glad to heal the wounded and rescue the dying. He advocated the theory of nourishing Yin and was respected by his students for generations. He was also regarded as one of the Four Distinguished Doctors in the Jin and Yuan Dynasties.

九、永康⑧　Introduction of Yongkang

永康，古称丽州，相传，三国吴赤乌八年（公元 245 年）孙权之母因病到此进香，祈求"永保安康"。吴国太病愈，孙权大喜，遂赐名为"永康"，并单立为县。唐朝时曾擢升为州。1992 年，经国务院批准，撤县设市。

Lizhou (a beautiful state in China) was ancient name of Yongkang. According to the legend, when the mother of Sun Quan (the King of Wu Kingdom) was ill, she went on a pilgrimage to pray for the "forever well-being" in a temple in Yongkang. After she recovered, Sun Quan was very pleased. He then granted Yongkang for Lizhou. During the Tang Dynasty, Yongkang was promoted to state. In 1992, the State Council changed the county to city.

现辖 10 镇、4 街道和 1 个经济开发区。永康市境内的地貌形态主要为低山、丘陵、平原三种。低山占全境面积约 17 %，丘陵占约 44.3 %，平原占全境面积约 38.7 %。永康气候温和，四季分明，气候类型为亚热带季风气候。年平均气温 17.5 ℃，年平均日照时数为 1909 小时，无霜期 245 天，年平均降水量 1387 毫米。

It administrates 10 towns, 4 sub-districts and 1 economic-development zone. The landforms are mostly low mountains, hills and plains, among them, low mountains account for 17 %, hills 44.3 % and plains 38.7 %. Yongkang is situated in the subtropical monsoon climate area with warm weather and clear seasonal distinction. The annual temperature averages 17.5 ℃, the annual sunshine averages 1909 hours, the annual frost-free period averages 245 days and the annual rainfall averages 1387 millimeters.

五金产业久负盛名。永康素有春秋铸剑、唐铸铜铳的传统技艺，享有"府府县县不离康、离康不是好地方"的美誉。

The hardware industry of Yongkang enjoys a long standing reputation. It has long been known for its tradition of sword-casting skill of the Spring and Autumn Period and of bronze-gun-casting technique of the Tang Dynasty. Yongkang, being famous nationwide, enjoys a good reputation that every prefecture and county cannot develop without Yongkang and, it would never be a good place without Yongkang.

人文荟萃山川秀美。永康自古文风鼎盛，人才辈出。北宋清官胡则，宽刑薄赋，兴革使民，勤政廉政，做了许多利国利民的好事。南宋时期永康状元陈亮，其农商并重、义利并举的"事功"学说，成为浙江重商文化的思想启蒙。境内有国家重点风景名胜区方岩，朱熹、陈亮曾讲学论理的五峰书院，国家级历史文化名镇芝英镇，十八蝴蝶、锡雕为代表的民间艺术享誉海内外。

It has a galaxy of celebrities and beautiful landscapes. The custom of learning and writing has been prosperous since ancient times, and talented people come forth in large numbers. Hu Ze, an upright and honest official of the Northern Song Dynasty, made great contribution to the people and the country. He was clement on punishment and tax, promoted reform and motivated common people. Chen Liang, Zhuangyuan (top-one scholar) of the Southern Song Dynasty, developed the Practical School with an emphasis on agriculture and commerce and on morality and interest. As a whole, His thoughts enlighten the pro-business culture. The landscapes—the key national scenic spot Fangyan, Wufeng Academy where Zhu Xi and Cheng Liang gave lectures—and the folk culture—the famous national historical and cultural Zhiying Town, Eighteen-butterflies Dancing and tin-carving— are world famous.

注释：

① Source: http://www.tudou.com/programs/view/YurEZDq-olw/

② Source: http://www.wuch.gov.cn/zjwc/wcgk/xzqy/index.html 参考婺城区人民政府中文网站

③ Source：https://www.huoche.net/zhengfu_330703/ 参考金东区人民政府中文网站。

④ Source: http://www.dongyang.gov.cn/ 参考东阳市人民政府中文网站。

⑤ Source: http://www.lanxi.gov.cn/ 参考兰溪市人民政府中文网站。

⑥ Source: http://www.zjwy.gov.cn/zjwy/index.html 参考武义县人民政府网中文,中文部分有修改。

⑦ Source: http://www.yw.gov.cn/ 参考义乌市人民政府网。

⑧ Source: http://www.yk.gov.cn/html/index.htm 参考永康市人民攻府网。

第二章　婺学

Chapter Two Wu Learning

第一节　吕祖谦　Lv Zuqian

　　南宋以来读书之风兴起，书院林立。当时最为出名的是丽泽书院，是南宋四大书院之一，也是吕祖谦讲学会友之所。随着读书风气大盛，对书籍的需求也大大增加，南宋时期婺州已采用雕版印刷术，尤其以婺州城内双桂堂的雕版印刷最为出名。

　　Since the Southern Song Dynasty, civilians had become interested in reading, and many academies were set up. At that time, Lize Academy was most famous among the four academies at the Southern Song Dynasty. Lize Academy was also the place where Lv Zuqian made speeches and met friends. Because of such a tendency, the demand of books were greatly increased. In the Southern Song Dynasty, block printing was used in Wuzhou. for block printing Shuang Gui Tang was most famous.

　　吕祖谦，他生于金华，人称"小东莱先生"，与朱熹、张栻并称"东南三贤"，南宋以来在金华讲学，因其讲学宽容并包、接纳各方学者而享盛誉，被尊称为婺学宗师。

　　Lv Zuqian, born in Jinhua, was named as "Mr. Young Donglai" , who was one of the "Three Talents in the Southeast" (Zhu Xi and Zhang Shi). In the Southern Song Dynasty, Lv Zuqian began to make speeches in Jinhua. Later, he became so famous for his speeches covering different topics that kinds of scholars from all plasces were Welcomed to attenhd his speech. He was awarded the honor of "Grand Master of Wu-Learning".

吕祖谦出生于 1137 年，出生于婺州。他的祖上八代曾出过 17 位进士、5 位宰相。高祖吕希哲（1039—1116），自其以下，包括曾祖吕好问、伯祖吕本中、祖父吕弸中、父吕大器等，皆为朝廷命官。如此一代一代连续不断地在朝为官，在宋以前和以后的历朝中不多见。

Lv Zuqian was born in Wuzhou in 1137. There were totally 17 *Jinshi* and 5 prime ministers among his grandfathers. His great-great-grandfather Lv Xizhe（1039—1116）, great grandfather Lv Haowen, grand uncle Lv Benzhong, grandfather Lv Pengzhong and father Lv Daqi were all governmental officials, which is uncommon in history.

吕祖谦少儿时期曾经跟随父亲在福建为官，他曾经师从林之奇、汪应辰、胡宪游，这几位都是宋朝的文学家。后面师从于他的伯祖吕本中。当时，学人多称其伯祖吕本中（1084-1145）为"东莱先生"，吕祖谦则称为"小东莱先生"。到了后世，一般均称吕祖谦为"东莱先生"。学业上吕祖谦受吕本中的影响最大。

In his childhood, Lv Zuqian followed his father who held an official position in Fujian. He learned from litterateurs Lin Zhiqi, Wang Yingchen and Hu Xianyou of the Song Dynasty, and later from his grand uncle Lv Benzhong (1084-1145). Lv Zuqian was known as "Mr. Young Donglai" for the largest impact from Lv Benzhong renowned as "Mr. Donglai".

吕祖谦的曾祖父吕好问携全家避难南迁，到婺州，他的祖父吕弸中（吕本中弟弟）始定居金华。1161 年，吕祖谦 25 岁，他的祖父吕弸中想给他官职，让他在严州桐庐县尉，主管学事，但是他没有去上任，偏偏要去参加科举考试。两年后，吕祖谦考中博学宏词科，接着又中进士。因为两门都中了，朝廷也特授他左从政郎（八品官员）。

His great grandfather Lv Haowen with family members took refuge southward and migrated to Wuzhou. His grandfather Lv Pengzhong (Lv Benzhong's younger brother) settled down in Jinhua. In 1161, Lv Pengzhong intended to provide him with an official post in charge of learning which was named Xianwei of Yanzhou Tonglu (an official just below the head of the county) at his 25. However, he declined it and attended the imperial examination. After two years, he stood out of the examination on profound knowledge and graceful letters, and then of the examination to be *jinshi*, which gifted him with Left Official in Politics (ranking eighth in ancient China official system) by the royal court.

但是命运多舛。在吕祖谦中进士的前一年，他妻子去世，儿子夭折。四年后，母亲去世，下葬于婺州，吕祖谦为母亲守丧，只能留在婺州教书。1169 年，也就是离母亲去世 3 年后，他再娶韩氏（为原配之妹），并到严州任所。干道六年（1170 年），他升任太学博士，并兼国史院编修官。但是次年，妻子韩氏又去世，女儿夭折。到了第二年（1172 年）他的父亲去世，他又为父亲守丧三年，这三年他依然教书写著作为主。淳熙三年（1176 年），守丧期满，因李焘的推荐，升任秘书省秘书郎，并兼国史院编修官与实录院检讨官。这一年，他 40 岁，身体健康状况已经大不如前，疾病缠身。淳熙四年（1177 年），他又娶芮氏为妻，2 年后其妻芮氏又去世，这一年他 42 岁。到了 1181 年，吕祖谦病故，享年 45 岁。

However, fate is unpredictable. In the year before he got the title of *jinshi*, his wife passed away and his son died young. Four years later, his mother passed away and was buried in Wuzhou where Lv Zuqian taught students in order to keep mourning. In 1169 (3 years after his mother's death), he married lady Han, who is ex-wife's younger sister, and undertook a position in Yanzhou. In 1170, he was promoted to Boshi (an official) in the imperial college, the editor of the National History Center and the Record Center. Nevertheless, his second wife died and his daughter died young. In 1172, his father departed. He kept mourning for three years. In 1176 (the third year of Chunxi period), he was editor and reviewer of the National History Center and the Record Center respectively. he was getting worse in health and was eaten up with diseases at age of 40. In 1177 (the fourth year of Chunxi Period), he married lady Rui who died two years later. In 1181, he died of illness at 45.

吕祖谦与他的家人一起葬在金华市武义县白洋街道上陈村明招山上。在吕祖谦墓的周围,还有其曾祖吕好问、伯祖吕本中、祖父吕弸中、父吕大器、母曾氏夫人、原配韩氏、继室芮氏的坟墓等十多座吕氏族人的墓地家族墓地分布于小范围内,相互距离很近,在南方较为少见。1989 年公布为浙江省文物保护单位, 2013 年 5 月公布为第七批全国重点文物保护单位。

Lv Zuqian and his family members were buried on Mingzhao Mountain in Shangchen Village of Baiyang Street, Wuyi county city, Jinhua. A dozen of tombs where Lv Zuqian, his great-grandfather Lv Haowen, grand uncle Lv Benzhong, grandfather Lv Pengzhong, father Lv Daqi, mother Ms Zeng, the first wife Ms Han and the third wife Ms Rui were buried are closely distributed in a small field, which is seldom in southern China. In 1989, these tombs were listed in Zhejiang Cultural-relics protection units. In May of 2013, they were listed in the seventh National Cultural-relics protection units.

第二节 婺学 Wu Learning

一、婺学总概 A Profile of Wu Learning

由吕祖谦创建的"婺学",在当时有相当影响。他的婺学得于家学,与北宋中原学术有着传承、授受的关系,与儒学一脉相承。与朱熹的"理学"、陆九渊的"心学"齐名,吕祖谦与朱熹、张栻过从甚密,时人以"东南三贤"目之。他又与浙东诸子及江西三陆子(陆九龄、陆九韶、陆九渊）私交也很深，朱熹和陆九渊的"鹅湖之会"，发起者就是吕祖谦。朱熹与陆九渊分别是客观唯心主义与主观唯心主义的代表。朱熹强调"格物致知"，认为格物就是穷尽事物之理，致知就是推致其知以至其极。并认为，"致知和格物只是一事"，是认识的两个方面。主张多读书，多观察事物，根据经验，加以分析、综合与归纳，然后得出结论。陆氏兄弟则从"心即理"出发，认为格物就是体认本心。主张"发明本心"，心明则万事万物的道理自然贯通，不必多读书，也不必忙于考察外界事物，去此心之蔽，就可以通晓事理，所以尊德性，养心神是最重要的，双方争议了三天，陆氏兄弟略占上风，最终不欢而散。

Wu Learning created by Lv Zuqian was considerablely influential at that time. It derived from his family schooling, interconnected with the Central China academy of the North Song Dynasty, and came down in the one continuous line with Confucianism. Wu learning enjoyed equal popularity with Neo-Confucianism of Zhuxi and School of Mind of Lu Jiuyuan. Lv Zuqian, Zhu Xi and Zhang Shi who kept a close relationship were renowned as "Three Celebrities in the Southeast". Besides, he maintained a deep friendship with learned scholars in East Zhejiang, and kept an intimate relationship with three philosophers surnamed Lu (Lu Jiuling, Lu Jiushao and Lu Jiuyuan). "The E-Hu-Temple Debate" between Zhu Xi and Lu Jiuyuan was arranged by Lv Zuqian. The philosophy of Zhu Xi and the Lu Jiuyuan advocated objective idealism and subjective idealism respectively. The former emphasized "Gewu Zhizhi" (investigation of things to obtain knowledge). Gewu is to investigate the truth of things thoroughly. Zhizhi is to obtain perfect knowledge by investigation. He reckoned that "Zhizhi and Gewu is one thing" and is also two aspects of cognition. He proposed to read more and observe better, and proposed analysis, synthesis and induction based on experience to get conclusion. The latter taking the perspective of "Mind is li" contended that Gewu is to investigate and identify with the inner Mind. Lu brothers claimed "exploring the inner Mind and manifesting li ". A clear Mind can lead to a nature Truth. People don't need to read and observe the external thing. Only they wipe out obstacles of the Mind, can they obtain li. Therefore, it is also essential to treasure inner virtues and cultivate thoughts. After three days' debate, the Lu brothers were in a slightly upper hand, leaving a displeasure with Lv Zuqian.

　　吕祖谦一生长期从事教育活动,从其学者甚众,朱熹、张栻这些大儒兼教育家都乐意把子女送到吕祖谦门下就学。在其弟弟吕祖俭的协助下,吕祖谦创建了与岳麓书院齐名气的丽泽书院,培养了大批学者,一直影响到明代的学风。

　　Lv Zuqian had a long career in education, and cultivated numerous students. Many learned scholars and educationists such as Zhu Xi and Zhang Shi would like to send their children to Lv Zuqian for acquiring knowledge. With assistance of Lv Zujian, his younger brother, Lv Zuqian built Lize Academy which is equally famous with Yuelu Academy, and he cultivated a multitude of scholars, which influenced social education till the Ming Dynasty.

二、婺学特点　Features of Wu Learning

　　包容、融合。宽宏容量、兼收并蓄。将不同内容、不同性质的理论都接收进来。

　　Wu Learning is magnanimous, confluent, generous and all embracing, it intends to incorporate theories of diverse schools.

表现形式 Presentation

"理""心"兼容 Li and Mind

　　"理"是吕祖谦思想体系的最高范畴,这与朱熹一致,但是吕祖谦将心学与理学并列起来说。"理"是自然规律、万物规则,"心"是天命。吕祖谦认为,理学和心学不要互相攻击,应该采取包容的态度。他认为通过人为努力妄想改变命运的人是不明理、不受命的行为。吕祖谦把主观与客观抬到了同一个高度。

Li is the highest category of his philosophy, which is identical with Zhuxi. Lv Zuqian discussed the Theory of Mind and the Neo-Confucianism at the same level. "Li " is the natural law and "Mind" is the fate. He contended that the two theories should embrace each other instead of attacking on both sides, and men who attempt to change fate through efforts don't understand Li and follow fate. He promoted subjectivity and objectivity to the same level.

功利兼容 Incorporation of utility

南宋学派理学和心学争论一直未果。吕祖谦意识到这样的争辩对于当时的统治没有实际益处,于是引进了功利之学来达到经世致用的目的,并且把功利之学大胆地和"理""心"融合在一起。

Lv Zuqian realized that the vain debate between the two philosophies in the South Song Dynasty was adverse to the government. He thus introduced the theory of utility so as to apply practical knowledge to manage state affairs. He creatively incorporated utility into " Li" and " Mind ".

吕祖谦的学说一个显著的特点就是"经世致用",这个学说避免了谈道德性命沦于空谈,"理""心"为理论,最终要落在实处。从生活中遇到的问题,学习新的知识来解决,就这样相互促进学习,逐步加深自己的理论知识与实践应用。

"The concept of practical knowledge of managing state affairs" , one remarkable thought of Lv Zuqian, put *Li* and Mind into practice rather than talk about them in vain. Men should utilize new knowledge to solve problems in life and help each other for mutual promotion in theory and application.

首先强调读史。重视史学,重视文献。从历史经典里面学到经验教训以对待当代事物。吕祖谦认为从博览圣贤书里面获得学问并运用于实际,研读历代典章制度可以直接涉及当时民生,寻找治民方针。在当时最能实现经世致用的是入仕,所以吕祖谦一生为官二十多年。

In the first place, it highlighted on reading history, appreciating historiography and document as well as learning experience and acquire knowledge from historical classics to deal with contemporary affairs. Lv Zuqian reckoned that the knowledge acquired from letters of men of virtues could be applied in life. Studying the ancient laws and regulations of dynasties could be beneficial to seeking measures of managing people. The best way to realize the concept of practical knowledge of managing state affairs is to be in politics, and that is why Lu Zuqian was in office for 20 years.

其次,经世致用运用于经济与教育等各个领域。当时经济生产力低下,安定民心需要给老百姓实际的利益,例如分田等。

In the second place, the concept was applied in fields like economy and education, etc. The economical productivity was rather low at that time, the government should provide with actual benefits (such as field distribution and practical education) to calm the public.

吕祖谦致力于对各种学术的调和,融会贯通。在此之前,各家分歧,邀约讲学的氛围不浓。在他之后,学术界学派逐渐明朗起来。

Lv Zuqian was engaged in reconciling and incorporating all learnings. The lecturing from schools of diverse thoughts was rare before but increasingly frequent at and after his time.

吕祖谦之后,婺学的传承,主要是"北山四先生",（即同是出生于金华的何基、王柏、金履祥和许谦）。他们认为"明理躬行,兼容并包,学以致用",用现在的话说就是实践是检验真理唯一的标准。陈亮是永康学派的代表人物,认为"理欲统一,王霸并行",就是说他们承认客观规律的存在,认为道义是不能脱离功利的,否则就是空谈。

After Lv Zuqian, Wu learning was mainly inherited by "Four Gentlemen in Beishan" (He Ji, Wang Bai, Jin Lvxiang and Xu Qian, who were all born in Jinhua). They firmly stuck to the ideology "be rational, be practical, be tolerant and be acceptable". Today, this ideology can be explained in this way —practice is the only test of truth. Chen Liang was a representative of Yongkang School, who held the ideology "rules are objectively existed, morality shall not be separated from material gains. if it is not, everything is nothing".

朱丹溪，师从北山四先生之一的许谦，义乌人，43岁时转医学。因其治病往往一帖药便见效，人称"朱一帖"，创立了滋阴学派，对中国医学贡献卓著。后人将他和刘宗素、张从正、李东垣一起被誉为"金元四大医家"，著有《局方发挥》《格致余论》。丹溪学说对朝鲜日本的影响也很大，日本建有丹溪学社。

Zhu Danxi, born in Yiwu, decided to study medicine at the age of 43, under the guidance of Xu Qian (one of the Four Gentlemen in Beishan). As he could cure the patient by only one dose of medicine, he was awarded the honor "Zhu Yitie" (Yitie means one packet of medicine). He created Ziyin School and made great contributions to Chinese medicine. Zhu Danxi, Liu Zongsu, Zhang Congzheng and Li Dongyuan were honored as "Four Great Medical Scientists in the Jin and Yuan Dynasties". He wrote *Ju Fang Fa Hui* and *Ge Zhi Yu Lun*. Danxi's theory greatly influenced North Korea and Japan, and in Japan, there is a Danxi School.

第三章　金华名人

Chapter Three Jinhua Celebrities

　　金华位于浙江中部,文化灿烂,名人辈出。金华文学和艺术充分体现了婺文化独特的魅力,比如唐初的骆宾王,其《咏鹅》被广为传颂,20世纪末的黄宾虹因其在风景画上的深厚影响,被誉为"中国人民的伟大画家"。金华著名诗人艾青以一首诗歌《大堰河,我的保姆》震惊国人。金华名人思想各异,是这座古老而日新月异的城市中璀璨文化的代表。

　　Jinhua, located in the central Zhejiang Province, has bright culture and numerous celebrities. Literature and arts in Jinhua have shown unique charming thoughts. Early in the Tang Dynasty, Luo Binwang's *Ode to the Goose* has been read widely all over the country. In the late 20th century, Huang Binhong has been awarded the title of "Outstanding Painter of the Chinese People" because of his profound influence on landscape painting. Ai Qing, another great man in Jinhua, astonished everyone in China with his poem *Dayanhe:My Nurse*. Every celebrity presents different delights of Jinhua and forms a part of bright culture in this historic but dramatic city.

第一节　古代文人墨客 Celebrities in Ancient Times

傅翁[①] Fu Xi

三国南北朝时期,意识形态由儒入玄,由玄入佛。傅大士生活在佛教寺院最盛的时期。经过佛经的大量翻译,佛理渐入中国化。日本学者忽滑谷快天指出:"梁武帝时代,僧副、慧初等,息心山溪,重隐逸,小乘之弊犹未能去。独傅翁超悟大乘,出入佛老,感化及于后世禅教者,翁一人也。"说明傅大士在佛教中国化过程中的作用。佛教要中国化,离不开中国本土的"道"和"儒",尤其是儒学影响很大。南北朝时范缜的《神灭论》,坚持"形神相即",与佛教"形神相异"对抗。所以佛教要在中国落地生根,难度是很大的。梁武帝用行政命令宣扬佛教,给佛教大开方便之门。不过即使如此,佛教要发展也离不开中国文化的儒、道之根基,要和它们互相融合,互相吸收。

During the Three Kingdoms and the Southern and Northern Dynasties, the ideology developed from Confucianism to myth and then to Buddhism. Fu Dashi lived in a period when the Buddhist temples prospered at peak. The great amount of translated sutras contributed to the localized Buddhism in China. The Japanese scholar Kaiten Nukariya said, "in the period of the Emperor Wu in the Liang Dynasty, Sengfu, Huichu and others cultivated in mountains and along rivers and lived in seclusion, which could not wipe off disadvantages. Only Fu Xi who comprehended Mahayana and researched and reflected on Buddhism and Taosim could influence and moralize later Zenists." This remark demonstrates the influence of Fu Xi on the localization of Buddhism that can't separate from Chinese Taosim and Confucianism (Confucianism is more influential). Fan Zhen of the Northern and Southern Dynasties in his *Theory of Spiritual Perish* stated the oneness of body and soul while Buddhism reckoned diversity of body and soul, from which,

Buddhism was supposed to develop in difficulties at that time. The Emperor Wu of the Liang Dynasty promoted Buddhism through administrative forces so as to give convenience to Buddhism development. But even still, Buddhism development should integrate and assimilate with Confucianism and Taosim as the roots of Chinese culture instead of deviating from them.

　　傅大士创导三教合一，楼颖著的《傅大士录》中也讲得很清楚：大士一日顶冠、披衲、跣履。帝问："是僧耶？"士以手指冠。"是道耶？"士以手指履。帝曰："是俗耶？"士以手指袖衣，遂出。故今双林寺塑大士像。顶道冠，身袈裟，足跣履，仿此迹也。

　　Fu Dashi initiated the oneness of Buddhism, Confuciansm and Taosim, which is clearly recorded in Lou Ying's Book of *Fu Dashi*. One day, Dashi wore a cap, mafors and walking slippers. The emperor asked, "Are you a monk?", Dashi pointed at his Taoist cap, "Are you a Taoist?", Dashi pointed at his confucianist slippers, "Are you a layfolk?", Dashi pointed at his mafors. And then Dashi went away. Since then, the statue of Fu Dashi in the Shuanglin Temple wears Taoist cap, Buddhist mafors and confucian shoes.

　　南怀瑾先生说："傅大士以道冠、僧服、儒履的表相，表示中国禅的法相，是以‘儒行为基，道学为首，佛学为中心的真正精神，配上他一生的行径，等于是以身设教，亲自写出一篇三教合一的绝妙好文。"

　　Nan Huaijin said, "the very truth from his clothing of Taoist cap, Buddhist mafors and Confucian shoes demonstrates the wears of Chinese Zen which is based on Confucianism, led by Taoism and centered on Buddhism" and his actions are to set himself as a marvelous example to advocate the oneness of three religions.

　　儒学是人世的学问，以做人治世为目的，便以"格物、致知、诚意、正心、修身、齐家、治国、平天下"为己任。至于学佛修道也离不开人世间，而且这是做人立身处世的基础，但是没有佛家的慈悲心肠是不能容物的。"有容德乃大，无欲性则刚"至于道家讲清净无为，宁静致远，理论少而智术多，没有道家的脑筋，很难制服一些混世魔王，他们从无为中显现有为,利于逆取,所以人们说:"开国以道,治国由儒。"这些都是"世间法",而佛家是要出世的,要了脱生死,超凡入圣。所谓三教合一,是指要有佛家的慈悲,用道家的智术和儒家的伦理,才不会走入偏激的途径。傅大士时代形成的中国文化,千百年来一直支配着中国的社会和中国人的意识形态。

Confucianism is the living knowledge aiming to conduct oneself and manage others, setting oneself to investigate things, pursue knowledge, conduct honesty, rectify mind and to cultivate your own family and rule the world. To practice Buddhism is to connect the life as the core. A man without a Buddhist mercy cannot tolerate others. "Greatness lies in the generosity, power lies in the few wants". Taoism lays emphasis on quietness and serenity. The highlight in intellectual trickery instead of theory can subdue these greatest devils. They use Taoism to undertake great actions from inaction. It is therefore said that Taoism helps found a country while Confucianism helps govern a country. As for Buddhism, it is to renounce the world, transcend worldliness and attain holiness. The oneness of three religions is to hold mercy of Buddhism, intellectual trickery of Taoism and ethics of Confucianism to lead a correct way of life. The Chinese culture developed from the period of Fu Dashi has administrated Chinese society and Chinese ideology for thousands of years.

傅大士合并三家为一家的主张,在我国历史上,确曾发生过重大的影响,甚至是我国传统文化精髓中的一部分。

The oneness of three religions merged by Fu Dashi made a significant influence in history, and can be regarded an essence of Chinese culture.

骆宾王[②]　Luo Binwang

骆宾王(约638–684),字观光,唐代著名诗人,生于婺州(今浙江金华义乌),在山东长大,与卢照邻、王勃和杨炯合称"初唐四杰"。

Luo Binwang (619–684), with courtesy name Guanguang, was a Chinese poet of Tang dynasty. His family was from Wuzhou (now Yiwu,

Zhejiang). But he was raised in Shandong. Luo is grouped with Lu Zhaolin, Wang Bo and Yang Jiong as the Four Paragons of the Early Tang, the most outstanding poets at that time.

据说,骆宾王六岁就能背诵诗歌。成年后,在道王李元庆府任职,其为当时执政的唐高宗的叔叔,665 年之后在当时首都长安任职。 670 年,他因事被放逐到新疆,之后又随军前往云南,后来他在身为洮州(今青海海东市)知府的裴行俭将军处任职军事通信,但他和裴的关系不好。最后,骆宾王成了长安县的官府秘书,官阶较低,但是地理位置好。

It was said that Luo Binwang could recite poetry when he was six years old. In adulthood, after a period serving for Daowang Li Yuanqing, an uncle of ruling Emperor Tang Gaozong, Luo worked in the central government in Chang'an from 665 A.D.. In 670 A.D., he was exiled to Xinjiang, then he travelled to Yunnan with the army. He later served for the prominent general Pei Xingjian while Pei was serving as the commandant at Tao Prefecture (roughly modern Haidong City, Qinghai), and was in charge of the military correspondences, but he did not maintain a good relationship with Pei. Eventually, Luo became a secretary at the government of Chang'an County— a low position but fairly prestigious due to its location at the capital.

678 年,骆宾王因多次上书讽刺武则天被撤职关押,但在一年后被释放。唐高宗死后,他的妻子武太后(后称武则天)摄政,太子中宗上位,不过很快被废,然后睿宗上位。骆宾王多次上书请柬,她不接受,于是在 684 年他又被降为临海县的文令。他和一批同样贬官在扬州的官员一起拥护李敬业为领袖,在扬州起兵反对武则天,拥护唐中宗复位。骆宾王负责起草讨伐檄文,他写了一份特别尖锐的声明反对武则天,即著名的《讨武氏檄》。

In 678 A.D., Luo Binwang was dismissed and imprisoned for satirizing Wu Zetian, but was released the following year. After Gaozong of Tang Dynasty died, his wife Wu Zetian was regent over her son Emperor Zhongzong who was quickly deposed, and then Emperor Ruizong. Luo made a number of suggestions to her, which she did not accept, and he was in turn demoted to the post of secretary general of Linhai County in 684 A.D. He and a number of similarly demoted officials met at Yang Prefecture (roughly modern Yangzhou, Jiangsu), and they, supported Li Jingye the Duke of Ying as their leader, rose against Empress Dowager Wu at Yang Prefecture, claiming their goal of Emperor Zhongzong's restoration. Luo was in charge of the resistance forces' correspondences, and he wrote a particularly sharp-worded declaration against Empress Dowager Wu.

据说,当武则天看到檄文的时候,非常轻蔑。然而,当她读到"一抔之土未干,六尺之孤何托?"时,她变得非常严肃。她说:"有这样的人才不用,是宰相的过错。"李敬业战败后一年后,据说骆宾王也被杀害,但武后为他的文采折服,令人收集出版其作品。还有人说他没死,藏身于杭州灵隐寺中。

It was said that when Empress Dowager Wu read the declaration, she smiled and laughed. However, when she reached the portion that, "The soil on the new imperial tomb is not yet dry, and to whom can the two-meter-tall orphan be entrusted?" She turned solemn and commented, "It is the fault of the chancellor that we lost this man's service." After Li Jingye's defeat later that year, it was said that Luo was also killed, but Empress Dowager Wu, impressed with his writing, sent people to gather them and publish them. It was also said he wasn't killed in fact, but hid in Lingyin Temple in Hangzhou.

在散文方面,他是一个骈文风格大师。他的诗歌往往同样复杂。他的作品也有长篇自传体叙事诗,但他最出名的是他的《咏鹅》,相传是他在七岁的时候写的。

As for prose, he was a master of the ornate "parallel prose" style. His poems are often similarly complex. Among his works, long autobiographical verse narrative also exists, but he is best known for his poem "*Ode to the Goose*", which was written when he was seven years old reputedly.

李清照[3] Li Qingzhao

第三章　金华名人　Chapter Three Jinhua Celebrities

李清照（1084–1155），自号易安居士，济南章丘（今属山东）人。她的一生既享受过幸福，也经历过苦难。前半生与赵明诚婚姻美满，诗词酬唱，共同收集整理金石文物，生活舒心适意；靖康之难后，家破夫亡，受尽劫难和折磨。因此，李清照的词作前后呈现出截然不同的风格与心境。前期词作主要传达少女天真烂漫的情怀以及少妇淡淡的离愁别绪，或者是表达对自然景物的热爱，对花草禽鸟的热爱。后期词作由轻盈妙丽的望夫词变成沉重哀伤的生死恋歌，词境由明亮轻快变成灰冷凝重，真切地反映了时代的苦难。

Li Qingzhao (1084–1155), self-titled Yi'an Jushi, was a native of Zhangqiu, Jinan (in the present-day Shandong Province). Her life was a bittersweet story. She married Zhao Mingcheng and shared with him the love of poetry and antiquities. They had enjoyed a happy family life before emperors of the Song Dynasty were captured by the invasive Jin people. In the midst of the Jin's invasion, her husband died and she had to flee from her sacked hometown. Hardship and suffering made her poetic style widely different from earlier works, which mainly deliver the maiden naivety and the subtle feelings of parting with her husband, or her passion with mother nature and her love of plants and pets. Then it turned to be melancholy and imposing, reflecting the hardship she bore.

理论上，李清照从词的本体论出发确立了词的独特地位，提出了"词别是一家"之说，认为词对音乐性和节奏感有更独特的要求，是与诗不同的抒情文体；创作中，她用最平常、最简单的语言来表现微妙复杂的心理和多变的情感流程。她的语言独具特色，无论口语还是书面语，一经她提炼熔铸，即别开生面，精妙清亮，如"绿肥红瘦""人比黄花瘦""宠柳娇花""柳眼梅腮"等，都是她的独创。她曾在金华住过一段时间，期间基于游历的经历也创作了一些广为流传的作品。

Theoretically speaking, Li Qingzhao is credited with the establishment of Ci as a different genre, independent from other genres. She suggested that Ci should follow more melodic and rhythmic patterns, distinguishing itself with Shi. In practice, she excelled in using normal language to depict the subtle mentality and emotions of the characters in question. Her choice of images and words, no matter they are formal or informal, is unique and innovative. The following lines best illustrate her poetic creativity, "The red must be getting thin, while the green is becoming plump" "I dwindle, thin as a golden flower" "spoiled willows and coquet flowers" "willow-leave eyes and plum-colored cheeks". When Li was in Jinhua, she created a lot of popular works based on her experience of life and travel.

她出生于书香门第。家有藏书万千,她从小就受到良好的文学教育。她父亲在她幼时便鼓励她写诗,参加男诗人的聚会。17 岁时,她已有名气,诗作出版成册。

She was born in a family of scholar-officials. The family had a large collection of books, and Li was able to receive comprehensive education in her childhood. Her father had encouraged her to write poetry from an early age and attend male poetic gatherings. And she was already famous and published works when she was 17.

1101 年,她嫁给了在开封书院就读的一名学生——赵明诚。他们那时经常来到位于开封城中心的大相国寺,流连于庭院中,用宣纸在寺中题词上拓片。婚后,两人共同致力于金石书画的搜集整理。他们虽然生活不太富裕,但志趣相投,生活美满。这也激发她早期创作了很多描写爱情的作品。

In 1101, she married a student, named Zhao Mingcheng, from Kaifeng Academy. And they spent a lot of time there in the great old Buddhist temple in the middle of town, wandering its courtyards and making ricepaper rubbings of its inscriptions. They shared interests in art collection and epigraphy after marriage. They were not particularly rich but shared enjoyment of collecting inscriptions and calligraphy which made their daily life valuable and they lived happily together. This inspired some of the love poems that she wrote.

第三章　金华名人　Chapter Three Jinhua Celebrities

宋钦宗靖康二年（1127 年），北方女真在金宋大战中攻破北宋首都开封。战祸始于山东，他们的家也被破坏殆尽。夫妻俩带着大部分家什奔赴南京，只在南京待了一年。1129 年丈夫赵明诚逝于赴任途中，这对李清照是个致命打击，至此再无复原。李清照在其丈夫出版的著作《金石录》后序中描写了她的婚姻生活和颠沛流离的生活，而她早期的词刻画了上层社会女子无忧无虑的日子，以优雅清润为主要特色。

The Northern Song's capital Kaifeng fell in 1127 to the Jurchens during the Jin–Song wars. Fighting took place in Shandong and their house was burned. The couple took many of their possessions when they fled to Nanjing, where they lived for a year. Zhao died in 1129 on the way to an official post. The death of her husband was a cruel strike from which Li never recovered. Li described her married life and the turmoil of her flight in an afterword to her husband's published work, *Jin Shi Lu*. Her earlier poetry portrays her carefree days as a woman of upper class, and is marked by elegance.

接着，李清照随南宋朝廷战后定都南方，最终定居杭州。在此期间，她继续词的创作。同时她还继续着丈夫赵明诚《金石录》著作的后期编撰工作，该书主要记录铭文款识和碑铭墓志等石刻文字，还录入了两人对早期作品的记录和评述。根据现在的记录，李清照短暂地和张汝舟有过一段婚姻，此人对她很差，没过几个月就离婚了。

Li subsequently settled in Hangzhou, where the Song government made its new capital after the war against the Jurchens. During this period, she continued writing poems. She also kept working on completing the book *Jin Shi Lu*, which was originally written by Zhao Mingcheng. The book was mainly about the calligraphy on bronze ware and stones. *Jin Shi Lu* also mentioned the documents Li and Zhao collected and viewed during the early period. According to some contemporary records, she was married to a man named Zhang Ruzhou for a short time who treated her badly, and she divorced him within months.

李清照是中国文学史上创造力最强、艺术成就最高的女性作家，她以女性的身份，真挚大胆地表现对爱情的热烈追求，丰富生动地抒写自我的情感世界，比"男子作闺音"更为真切自然。她的横空出世，改变了男子一统文坛的传统格局。

Li Qingzhao is believed to be the most prolific and accoplished female poet in the history of Chinese literature. Her audacity in expressing the pursuit of true love and delicacy in the depiction of emotions reflect her intuition of being a female. Her prominence in the Southern Song Dynasty unprecedentedly changed the male-dominated field of poetry.

最近在中国，女权视角的评论让我们了解了另外一个李清照。在男权社会中，她关系紧张的婚姻，这个才华横溢的女人想要发声，谈论她的内心和生活，谈论公众和政治。因为写诗，她遭到一些人的指责。女人是不应该写诗的，这是男人的工作，而诗歌是男人社交的主要方式之一。男人会在一起喝酒，然后共同作诗。一个作前两句，另一个接后两句，通过这样进行创作。女人也可以参与，但大多是欢场女子。得体的女性是不参加男性的作诗集会的。她们也会写诗，但能否出版又是另一回事了。宋代对于女性来说是个矛盾的时期，一方面这时期女性的声音可能是首次被听到，与此同时，缠足也开始流行起来。"女性可以享受高等教育，但是在男性主导的儒家社会里，为了社会和谐，女性必须对父亲、丈夫和国家保持忠贞。"保守派的先锋，历史学家司马光这样写道。

But recent feminist criticism here in China is giving us another view of her. The strains within her marriage in a society dominated by men, the ambitions of a brilliant woman to find a voice that was not only interior and personal, but also public and political. She was criticized by some people at the time for saying things, for writing poems. Women were not supposed to write poems. This was man's work. And poetry was one of the major ways of social interaction among men. Men would go and drink a cup of wine, and they would compose poem with each other. One would say two lines of a poem and the other would give the next two lines. They would create new poem in that way. Women could do this, but increasingly there were courtesans who did this. Respectable women didn't participate in this with men doing it. They still wrote, but the published is a different matter. Song Dynasty is a paradoxical period for women. For one thing, women's voice appeared strongly for the first time, and for another, foot binding started to become widespread. So "women could be highly educated, but to play their part in male-led Confucian society, women were to cultivate loyalty to father, husband and state to ensure national cohesion. "wrote by the leading conservative, the historian Sima Guang.

徐霞客④ Xu Xiake

徐霞客 (1587—1641),地理学家、旅行家和文学家,以勇敢谦逊著称。徐霞客祖籍江西,名宏祖,徐豫庵和王孺人的第二个儿子。徐霞客字振之。霞客是他的朋友陈继儒给他取的号,意思是"日落时彩霞中的人"。他的另外一个朋友黄道周也给他取了个号:霞逸,意思是"在日落时的彩霞中无拘无束"。受父亲影响,他喜爱读地理、探险和游记之类的书籍。人们也常说是他母亲的鼓励促成了徐霞客的爱好。

Xu Xiake (1587—1641) was a descriptive Chinese travel writer and geographer noted for his bravery and humility. With an ancestry in Jiangxi, he was born with a name of Hongzu, the second son of Xu Yu'an and Wang Ruren. His sobriquet is Zhenzhi. Xiake was an alternate sobriquet given to him by his friend Chen Jiru and it means "one in the sunset clouds". His another friend, Huang Daozhou, also gave him an alternate sobriquet Xiayi, meaning "untrammelled in the sunset clouds". Influenced by his father, he enjoyed reading books about geography, adventure, travelling and so on. It was also often commented that it was his mother's encouragement to travel that shaped Xu's predilections.

21 岁开始出游,30 年间足迹遍及现在的 16 个省区。他在调查研究中从不盲目轻信前人留下的文献总结。相反,他发现了前人在文献中记述的地理研究有很多谬误偏差。

From the age of 21, Xu Xiake began to travel around for thirty years he conducted surveys in 16 provinces, leaving his footsteps in virtually every part of the country. In conducting his surveys and investigations, he would never blindly embrace the conclusions recorded in previous documents. Instead, he discovered that the documentations made by his predecessors in their geographical studies were quite unreliable in many aspects.

徐霞客游历 30 年,写了 60 万字的游记。他花了很多年在西南地区考察。为了进行细致的考察,他很少乘车坐船,几乎全靠双脚翻山越岭。他去世后,这些游记经后人整理成书,就是著名的《徐霞客游记》。《徐霞客游记》主要记述了他在 1613 年至 1639 年游历期间的观察结果,提供了有关地理学、水文学、地质学和植物的详细记录,融地理学与文学于一书的《徐霞客游记》向来被看作一部奇人写的奇书。徐氏七次游浙,浙江是他涉足次数最多的省份。明崇祯九年 (1636 年) 他第七次游浙,写下了著名的《浙游日记》,这篇游记成为他整个游记中的重要篇章。《浙游日记》中对地方性的民情风俗多有所涉,在行文的三言两语中,含义深刻,语言简练,蕴含着丰富的社会生活内容。我们对它作注、作释、作解,有助于对其整个游记的社会价值的认识和理解,也有助于今天的旅游开发。作为文学作品,《徐霞客游记》于叙事过程中穿插生动的风景描写,具有强烈的现实意味,使用了动态的描述和象征,比原来的同类作品更加精致、更注意细节,具有很高的艺术价值和审美价值。而且,作者为了表情达意应用了大量的术语和修辞技巧。在记录旅游经历的同时,徐霞客还记下了少数民族的分布情况以及当地人民的生活和习俗,这些在正史里是很难见到的,所以《徐霞客游记》对研究历史和民族也很有价值。

Xu Xiake, after 30 years of traveling, wrote many travel diaries with a total of 600 000 characters. He visited southwestern China extensively for years. In order to carry out thorough investigations, he seldom traveled by carriage or boat. Instead, he took long trips on foot almost all the time, climbing mountains and hills. After his death, these diaries were compiled into a book called *Xu Xiake's Travel Notes*. The book is mainly about his observation during his travel from 1613 to 1639 and provides detailed records of geography, hydrology, geology and plants. *Xu Xiake's Travel Notes* has always been regarded as a unique literary and geographic book. Xu toured Zhejiang for seven times as his most favorite place. His *Zhejiang Travel Notes*, written on his seventh journey in 1636, makes up an important part in his *Travel Notes*. It records many of the local folklore and customs in very exact and meaningful albeit simple descriptions which reveal to us the social and cultural life of local inhabitants in this part of China. The study of his *Notes* may be helpful with a better understanding of life and a promotion of the tourist industry. As a literary work, the book vividly portrays the landscapes amid narration, hence imbuing it with a strong real-life flavor. Through applying dynamic description and personification, the travel diaries were more delicate and paid more attention to details than did their predecessors, boasting a high artistic and aesthetic value. Besides, a large glossary and rich rhetoric techniques were employed to express the author's feelings.While recording his travel experiences in his diaries, Xu Xiake also related the lives and customs of local people as well as the distribution of ethnic minority groups, which was seldom seen in official history. Hence, this book is also valuable in the study of history and nationalities.

李渔⑤　Li Yu

李渔，又名李笠翁，是中国剧作家、小说家和出版商。明末清初时期出生在如皋，在现今江苏省。他是著名的剧作家、戏剧理论家、作家，被誉为"东方莎士比亚""世界戏剧大师"和"中国戏曲理论之祖"。他同时也是一名园林设计师、化妆师、时装设计师、美食家、旅行者。他倡导文化休闲，懂得享受生活，如何娱乐，如何在快乐中赚钱。

Li Yu, also known as Li Liweng, was a Chinese playwright, novelist and publisher. Born in Rugao in the late-Ming and the early-Qing Dynasties, in present-day Jiangsu Province. He was a famous dramatist, a dramatic theorist and a writer who was honored as the "Oriental Shakespeare", "World Drama Master" and "The Ancestor of Chinese Drama Theory". He was also a garden designer, makeup artist, fashion designer, gourmet, traveler and he advocated the leisure of culture, and knews how to enjoy life, how to play, and how to make money while being happy.

虽然他通过了科举的院试,但是在接下来的乡试中失利,而后面对政治动荡不安的新王朝,转向商业创作。李渔是一个演员,制片人,导演和剧作家,与自己的戏班一起游历四方。他的戏剧《风筝误》仍然是中国人喜爱的昆曲曲目。他的自传作者称他为"企业型作家"和"当时最灵活、最进取的作家"。

Although he passed the first stage of the imperial examination, he did not succeed in passing the higher levels before the political turmoil of the new dynasty, but instead turned to writing for sale. Li was an actor, producer, and director as well as a playwright, who traveled with his own troupe. His play *Errors Caused by the Kite* remained a favorite of the Chinese Kun opera stage. His biographers called him a "writer-entrepreneur" and the "most versatile and enterprising writer of his time".

《肉蒲团》,这部精心设计的喜剧和经典的中国情色文学,正是出自李渔之手。他还写了一本短篇小说称为《十二楼》。当时,他的作品被广泛阅读,大家都欣赏他大胆创新的主题。他在《萃雅楼》里提到了同性恋问题。他在集子《无声戏》和《怜香伴》都有重提这个主题。

Li is the author of *The Carnal Prayer Mat*, a well-crafted comedy and a classic of Chinese erotic literature. He also wrote a book of short stories called *Twelve Towers*. In his time, he was widely read, and appreciated for his daringly innovative subject matter. He addressed the topic of *same-sex* love in the tale, *House of Gathered Refinements*. This is a theme which he revisits in the collection *Silent Operas* and his play *The Fragrant Companion*.

李渔也因为他的随笔或小品,以及美食著作而出名。林语堂欣赏李渔,并翻译了其大量随笔。李渔的散文《胃》极具创造性的讽刺意义,文中提出"嘴和胃是引起人类所有的烦恼的起源",又说,"植物可以没有嘴和胃存活,岩石和土壤可以没有补给而存在。那么为什么我们人类必须被赋予嘴和胃这两个额外的器官"？林还翻译了李的《如何富而富》《如何快乐地穷》《睡、行、坐、立的艺术》等，这些作品都展现了他对严肃话题的讽刺态度。

Li was also known for his informal essay, or *xiaopin*, and for his gastronomy and gastronomical writings. Lin Yutang appreciated Li and translated a number of his essays. Li's whimsical, ironic *On Having a Stomach* proposes that "the mouth and the stomach cause all the worry and trouble of mankind throughout the ages". He continued that the "plants can live without a mouth and a stomach, and the rocks and the soil have their being without any nourishment. Why, then, must we be given a mouth and a stomach and endowed with these two extra organs?" Lin also translated Li's *How to be Happy Though Rich* and *How to be Happy Though Poor*, and *The Arts of Sleeping, Walking, Sitting and Standing*, which illustrate his satirical approach to serious topics.

第二节　近现代文人志士 Celebrities in Modern Times

金华在近代历史上是一座饱经沧桑的城市。从辛亥革命开始，金华人民就一直踊跃在革命的前线。1900 年，金华 2 万多劳动人民成立了华龙会，成为革命进行活动宣传的重要阵地，也是浙中光复革命的大本营。龙华会创立不久，龙华会副会长张恭在金华、义乌一带农村成立戏班巡演。戏班主要演员都是龙华会的骨干分子，平时除了演戏，还从事联络会员、发展组织、传递情报、掩护同志和散发进步书刊等活动，是龙华会的一支重要力量。当时，光复会创始人陶成章伪装成风水先生跟随戏班活动，扩大群众基础。光复会领袖秋瑾与徐锡麟策划发动浙皖起义，多次来到金华与龙华会骨干密谈，以金华为光复会起义中心。

Jinhua has experienced great hardships and turbulence in the modern history. Since the 1911 Revolution (the Year Xinhai), Jinhua citizens had been active on the front-line of revolution. During that period, around 1900, over 20000 members of laboring people founded the Chinese Dragon Society, which became the main front for revolutionary campaigns and the headquarter for revolutionizing the central Zhejiang. After the foundation of Chinese Dragon Society, Zhanggong, the vice chairman, organized a theatrical troupe on tours in the villages of Jinhua and Yiwu. The main players of the troupes were core members of the Dragon Societys, besides the shows, they also engaged in activities like liaising with members, recruiting new members, passing on information, covering comrades and distributing progressive books and magazines. It was a significant force of the Dragon Society. At that time, Tao Chengzhang, the founder of the Restoration society, followed the tournament to expand popular support, disguised as a Master of Fengshui. Qiu Jin, one of the leaders of the Restoration Society, planned and launched the Zhejiang and Anhui Uprising together with Xu Xilin. She paid several visits to Jinhua to have private discussions with the core members of Chinese Dragon Society and set Jinhua as uprising center of the Restoration Society.

1904 年，金华的社会名流金兆銮、蔡汝霖、盛俊等与张恭的共同努力下创办了《萃新报》，是传播新思想新观念的文明报，也启迪了邵飘萍。

Cuixin Newspaper was founded by jointing efforts of celebrities in Jinhua in 1904, such as Jin Zhaoluan, Cai Rulin, Sheng Jun and Zhang Gong. It was a civilized newspaper that spread new ideas and new concepts, which had enlightened Shao Piaoping.

在抗日战争高潮中，金华出现很多用笔杆子战斗的革命者。陈望道翻译并出版了《共产党宣言》第一个中文全译本。一代报人邵飘萍是中国新闻理论的开拓者和奠基人。1918 年创办《京报》。同年，与蔡元培一起创办北京大学新闻学研究会，致力于新闻教育事业。1920 年后，开始宣扬马列主义，于 1924 年加入中国共产党，对共产主义运动做了大量报道。1926 年，邵飘萍被捕并惨遭杀害。施复亮也是早期活动家、领导者。

第三章　金华名人　Chapter Three Jinhua Celebrities

1920 年 3 月施复亮来到上海,参加了陈独秀自倡的马克思主义研究会。6 月底,全国最早的共产主义组织——上海共产主义小组成立,机关刊物就叫《共产党》,施复亮是发起人之一。

In the climax of the Anti-Japanese War, many revolutionists turned up in Jinhua fighting by writing. Chen Wangdao translated and published the first Chinese version of *The Communist Manifesto*. A great journalist, Shao Piaoping was pioneer and founder of the Chinese journalism theory. He founded *Peking Press* in 1918. In the same year, he and Cai Yuanpei founded the Seminar on Journalism in Peking University to concentrate on the cause of journalism education. He started to advocate Marxism-Leninism after 1920, joined the CPC in 1924, and made a great number of reports on communist movements. Shao was arrested and killed cruelly in 1926. Shi Fuliang was also one of the early activists and leaders. In March 1920, Shi came to Shanghai and joined in the Marxism seminar initiated by Chen Duxiu. In the end of June, Shanghai Communist Group-the earliest communist group in China was founded, the publication was called *Communist*. Shi was one of the founders.

1919 年 5 月 4 日,五四运动爆发。北京学生爱国大示威的消息传到金华,浙江省立第七中学、第七师范学校的学生首先响应,集结 2000 余人,游行示威,罢课一周。五四运动的浪潮下,《新青年》等进步刊物进入金华,马克思主义从学生、工人到各界人民,从城市到农村,遍及金华大地。

On May 4th 1919, the May Fourth Movement broke out. The news that Beijing students had organized a patriotic demonstration came to Jinhua, the students in the 7th Public Middle School of Zhejiang and the 7th Normal School responded firstly. They gathered over 2000 people to demonstrate and the strike went on for one week. With the tide of the May Fourth Movement, progressive publications like *New Youth* came to Jinhua, with Marxism spread to every corner of the land, from students and workers to all walks of life, from cities to villages.

1925 年夏,千家驹加入中国共产党,同年,钱兆鹏、章驹、刘文铭也加入共产党,建立中共金华支部。1926 年改名为中共金华独立支部,开展工农运动,支持革命军北伐,担负领导金华革命的重任。

In the summer of 1925, Qian Jiaju joined the CPC. In the same year, Qian Zhaopeng, Zhang Ju, Liu Wenming also joined CPC. Then Jinhua Branch of the CPC was established. In 1926, it was renamed Jinhua Independent Branch of CPC, to carry on workers' and peasants' campaign, to support the Northern Expedition, and shoulder the responsibility of leading Jinhua revolution.

金佛庄是浙江省东阳人。1922 年,加入中国共产党,1924 年参与创建黄埔军校,并在北伐战争中立下卓著战功。1926 年,金佛庄前往杭州策动起义的途中被捕。他是第一位牺牲在南京雨花台的共产党人。

Jin Fozhuang was from Dongyang, Zhejiang. He joined CPC in 1922. In 1924, he co-founded the Huangpu Military Academy and achieved brilliant victories in the Northern Expedition. In 1926, Jin was arrested on his way to Hangzhou to plan an uprising. He was the first CPC member killed in Yuhuatai, Nanjing.

近代也涌现出不少能人志士。他们用画笔、文学作品、严谨的科学态度表达了对这片土地的热爱。何炳松(1890—1946),字柏丞,浙江金华人,历史学家和历史教育家。何氏三杰之一,新史学的奠基人,曾经担任暨南大学校长,浙江省第一城市文化名人。

Modern Jinhua saw an emerging group of capable people with lofty ideals, who expressed their love to the country and the people through paintings, literary works and rigorous attitudes to science. He Bingsong (1890—1946), from Jinhua, Zhejiang, with a courtesy name of Bocheng, was a famous historian and educator. Reputed as one of the three greatest He people, he was founder of the new historical science. Once being the President of Jinan University, he was the most famous celebrity in the cultural sector in Zhejiang.

艾青是现代诗人，原名蒋海澄，1932年在上海加入左翼美术家联盟，不久被捕，在狱中写了《大堰河——我的保姆》，发表后引起了轰动。

Ai Qing, originally named Jiang Haicheng, was a famous modern poet. In 1932, he joined in the Left-wing Artists Union in Shanghai and was arrested shortly after. While in prison he wrote his book *Dayanhe: My Nurse*, which had made a big stir after publication.

黄宾虹是近现代画家，生于浙江金华。在中国现代绘画史上有"北齐南黄"之说，"北齐"指的是齐白石，"南黄"指的就是黄宾虹。黄宾虹成名较晚，早年受"新安画派"的影响，以干笔淡墨为主，称为"白宾虹"。50岁以后画风趋于写实。80岁以后才形成了人们熟知的"黑密厚重"的画风。90岁大寿那天，被国家授予"中国人民优秀画家"称号。

Huang Binhong, born in Jinhua, Zhejiang, was a modern painter and scholar. In modern Chinese painting history, there is a saying that "Qi in the north and Huang in the south". The former refers to Qi Baishi, while the latter is Huang Binhong. He became famous rather late. He was influenced by the"Painting School of Xin'an" when he was young, so his works featured with dry brush and light ink, which are called "White Binhong". After 50, his painting style shifted to realism. The well-known "forceful and profound style" came its way after he was 80. On his 90th birthday, Qi was entitled "Chinese Excellent Painter" by the government.

严济慈是我国著名物理学家，他在光谱学、应用光学和光学仪器、大气物理学等方面做出了杰出贡献，是中国光学仪器研制工作的奠基人。2012年，为了纪念严济慈为社会带来的贡献，国际将一颗永久编号的行星命名为"严济慈星"。

Yan Jici, a famous physicist in China, had made great contributions in spectroscopy, optics, optical instruments and atmosphere physics. He was a founder for production of optical instruments. In 2012, a permanently numbered star was named "the Star of Yan Jici" to commemorate his contributions to society.

施光南祖籍浙江金华，被称为"时代歌手"，是 1949 年以来中国自己培养的新一代作曲家。他先后创作《祝酒歌》《月光下的凤尾竹》《在希望的田野上》等脍炙人口的歌曲，他的父亲施复亮就是共青团早期领导人。

Shi Guangnan, from Jinhua Zhejiang, was regarded as "Singer of the Times". He was also one of the new-generation composers cultivated by China independently. He composed many classic hits one after another, including *A Toasting Song, The Hedge Bamboo in The Moonlight, On the Hopeful Field*. His father Shi Fuliang was one of the early leaders of the Communist Youth League.

黄宾虹⑥ Huang Binhong

传统国画是用毛笔涂上黑色墨水或彩色颜料在宣纸上绘画的艺术。从题材上看，中国画可以分为人物画、花鸟画和山水画三种类型。元代，四大画家——黄公望、倪瓒、吴镇和王蒙，代表了当时山水画的最高水平。他们的作品极大地影响了明清山水画。位于长江下游的苏州吴门画派在明代兴起。"八怪"就出自与之隔江相望的扬州，这八位画家都具有较强的人格特点：孤傲，拒绝向权贵屈服。他们用写意手法开阔了花鸟画的创作格局。以徐悲鸿为首的许多优秀画家也涌现出来。他们的作品是中西绘画风格的完美结合，吸收了西方古典主义、浪漫主义和印象主义。这一时期其他伟大的画家包括齐白石、张大千和黄宾虹。黄宾虹，作为一个写意山水画大师，值得被人熟知。

Traditional Chinese painting is an art of painting on a piece of Xuan paper with a Chinese brush that was soaked with black ink or colored pigments. By subject, traditional Chinese painting can be classified into three types: figure painting, flower-and-bird painting and landscape painting. During the Yuan Dynasty the "Four Great Painters" — Huang Gongwang, Ni Zan, Wu Zhen and Wang Meng — represented the highest level of landscape painting. Their works immensely influenced landscape painting of the Ming and Qing dynasties. The Ming Dynasty saw the rise of the Wumen Painting School, which emerged in Suzhou at the lower reaches of the Yangtze River. Yangzhou, which faces Suzhou across the Yangtze River, was home to the "Eight Eccentrics" -the eight painters all with strong characters, being proud and aloof, who refused to follow orthodoxy. They used freehand brushwork and broadened the horizon of flower-and-bird painting. Many outstanding painters, led by Xu Beihong, emerged, whose paintings recognized a perfect merging of the merits of both Chinese and Western styles, absorbing western classicism, romanticism and impressionism. Other great painters of this period include Qi Baishi, Zhang Daqian and Huang Binhong. Huang Binhong, as a master of freehand landscape painting, is worthy to be known.

　　黄宾虹（1865-1955），原籍安徽省徽州歙县，生于浙江金华，是一代中国美术史学家及文人画家。黄宾虹被誉为文人画风改革先驱者，以写意山水画为人熟知。其画作深受早期画家李流芳、程邃、程正揆及髡残等人的影响。黄宾虹从五岁开始学画，中年后他来到上海从事多年的画集编辑工作。直到 1948 年，他搬到杭州任教西湖艺术学院，才结束他在上海和北京任教生涯。

　　Huang Binhong (1865-1955) was a Chinese art historian and literati painter. His ancestral home was She County in Anhui Province, but he was born in Jinhua Zhejiang. He is considered one of the innovators in the literati style of painting and is noted for his freehand landscapes. His painting style showed the influence of the earlier painters Li Liufang, Cheng Sui, Cheng Zhengkui and Kun Can. Huang studied painting when he was 5 years and then, after middle age, he spent many years editing literary and art journals in Shanghai. Huang Binhong taught painting at fine arts colleges in Shanghai and Beijng until he moved to Hangzhou in 1948 where he taught at the West Lake Art College.

　　他还是写意山水画一代大师，从小精研临摹早期大师们的著作及绘画技巧。他钻研笔墨的运用，以干笔淡墨、疏淡清逸为特色，而到了晚年，黄宾虹的山水画以黑密厚重为特色,同时他的作品以遒劲有力的笔锋和新奇纵横的构图而见长。

He was also a master of freehand landscape painting and he was well versed in the works of the great masters of the past. Though he imitated many of their techniques, Huang Binhong experimented with the use of ink and stroke. He made achievements with shading and layering that have seldom been equaled, while in the late years, Huang Binhong made a simple yet profound achievement in his landscapes by the use of thick dark ink over which he applied light or heavy coloring. His work was also known for its powerful brushwork and its fresh approach to composition.

早年黄宾虹受"新安画派"影响,画作以干笔淡墨、疏淡清逸为特色,被称为"白宾虹";之后转学吴镇的积墨风格,以黑密厚重特色,渐渐形成浑厚有力的风格,该时期他被称为"黑宾虹"。在其晚年,他渐渐摆脱了"师古人"的影子,开始创立属于自己的风格,对山水画的运笔用墨进行深入研究。黄宾虹通过对中国艺术精神的深刻认识和探索体验,创立了"五笔法"和"七墨法"等运笔用墨理论;其山水画创作经历了"白宾虹""黑宾虹"和"创风格"三个时期,他巧妙运用积墨法,最终形成浑厚华滋的艺术风格,成为当代中国山水画之集大成者。1953年,在他的90岁寿辰上,黄宾虹被国家授予"中国人民优秀的画家"称号。

In the early years, Huang was under profound influence of Xin'an painting, which is called "White Binhong style" period because of its elegance, then Huang turned to learn Wu Zhen' style of Ji Mo illustration which is black, dense and thick and gradually formed a deep and vigorous style, In this period he was known as the "black Binhong style". In later period in his life he got rid of the shadow of the ancients and began to create his own style, researched the use of brush and ink on landscape painting. Huang founded the calligraphy ink theory of "Wubifa" and "Qimofa" through his deep understanding of Chinese art spirit and exploration experience. His landscape painting creation has experienced three periods of "white Binhong style" "black Binhong style" and "creation style" . He is clever in using Ji Mo method, and finally formed his artistic style of thickness and elegance, becoming a master of contemporary Chinese landscape painting. In 1953,on his 90th birthday, Huang Binhong was awarded the title of "Outstanding Painter of Chinese People."

黄宾虹在中国现代绘画史上是一位注重传统再发掘,努力以中国画内部破解进展难题的中国山水画画家,他的艺术实践对中国传统绘画向现代形态转换有着重要的启迪作用。在此以黄宾虹"引书入画"为主要线索,着重梳理书法对其山水画笔墨原因及时代转换的重要作用。黄宾虹以深厚的国学底蕴和对书法的独到洞见,从书法与绘画的点画结构中寻找到了"引书入画"的切入点,并以金石学中研发出的篆籀笔法来作为书法、绘画的笔法基础,以笔法正轨校正了以往绘画运用上的用笔舛误。黄宾虹的"引书入画"是从书法的法、理、意各层面展开的,他将考古学入于金石学,以金石学入于文字学,以文字学入于书学,再以书学入于画学,形成书学、画学回环互通的学术链条,最终完成了从书法向画法的转化。黄宾虹本着"学贵根柢、道尚贯通"的学术态度,在古人总结的书法原则基础上,将毛笔工具的空间运动形式,用笔法度和用笔品质,以及书法的功夫体认与审美内涵整合贯通,概括出可为绘画所用的"五笔七墨",使抽象的"引书入画"论述有了极强的现实操作性。为了使书法原则更直接地运用在山水画中,提升笔墨的内容蕴涵,黄宾虹将书法点画形态的"一波三折"同山水画中皴法形态的"一波三折"相融合,生化出既有书法意味,又有皴法形态的"点画笔触"。黄宾虹的"引书入画"不仅用书法来转变自己的绘画面目,而且着眼于用书法去消解中国传统山水画千百年来所形成的皴法、书法等法式垒块,使"点画笔触"在视觉感受和书法机制的双重统摄下,成为可自由运用的笔墨语汇。黄宾虹通过"引书入画",把中国山水画的用笔和用墨进行纯化和整合,丰富了笔墨的表现力,并将一味超脱的传统文人画笔墨落实在绘画主体感受下的自然现实中,使笔墨和自然、人生有了直接的联系。黄宾虹缘书法之力,把笔墨从传统法式、程式中解放出来,并顺应笔墨本体进展规律,将"笔墨合一"的单纯化语汇导入变化多端的画法中,为纯化后的笔墨体现提供了无限的进展空间,完成了从传统内部破解中国画现代进展的难题。黄宾虹的"引书入画"是在中西方绘画艺术参照下进行的,他不仅寻找到书法和绘画的契合点,而且还主动地寻找中西方绘画的契合点,积极吸收西方绘画的有益成分为我所用,把中国画纳入世界艺术进展格局中来考量。我们从黄宾虹"引书入画"的整个历程可以看出,书法形式资源对中国画当代进展具有现实作用,中国绘画是可以以民族方式完成从传统向现代转换的,中国绘画也完全有能力与世界绘画艺术平等对话。

Huang Binhong is a typical case in modern history of Chinese painting, who attaches importance to tradition and tries to solve the problem of development from within Chinese painting itself. His artistic practice contributes significant enlightenment to Chinese painting in its transformation from tradition to modernity. This dissertation centers around the clue of "drawing calligraphy into painting", puts much emphasis on the vital role of calligraphy in forming Huang's type of painting style. Based on his profound mastery of traditional culture and unique insight, and inspired by the structure of points and strokes in both calligraphy and painting, Huang defines the breaking point of drawing calligraphy into painting, and lays the epigraphic foundation of painting and calligraphy. He combines archaeology into epigraphy, epigraphy into philology, philology into calligraphy, and calligraphy into paintings. By an academic cycle, he finally concludes the transformation from calligraphy description to painting description. Huang Binhong sums up the principle of "five tips of a writing brush and seven tips of ink" by integrating the motion forms of brush, technique characteristic and the esthetic penetration, and etc. This principle adds much more operation ability to the abstract of the theory of "drawing calligraphy into painting". In order to utilize calligraphy more directly in Chinese landscape painting and enhance effects of its implication, Huang fuses the shape of "three waves to a single stroke" in calligraphy with the texture of rocks and mountains in the

Chinese landscape painting. In this way, calligraphy becomes an important part of the landscape painting. His theory of "drawing calligraphy into painting" not only changes the painting style, but also elements of description, and turns the structure of points and strokes into a language of free flow. Huang Binhong enriches the expression ability of description by refining and reorganizing the use of ink and brush, and he establishes description relationship between ink and nature. Huang Binhong liberated painting from the shackles of traditional formula, combined refined elements of description into his paintings, and completed modernization of the traditional Chinese painting, thus providing infinite space for the development of Chinese landscape painting. Huang Binhong's drawing calligraphy into painting also refers to fine arts of both China and western countries. He not only finds the integration of calligraphy and painting, but also makes great efforts to explore the resemblance between China and the west when they ttranscend material shape, doing his utmost to absorb the essence of western drawing. In this way, he has put Chinese painting into the perspective of overall pattern of cosmopolitan art development. From the course of drawing calligraphy into painting, it can be concluded that calligraphy is a great resource and has real influence on the development of Chinese painting, and that the Chinese painting has full capacity to accomplish modernity and dialogue with cosmopolitan art on an equal footing.

艾青　Ai Qing

艾青，原名蒋海澄，（1910 年 3 月 27 日出生中国浙江金华，1996 年 5 月 5 日去世于北京），是一位著名的诗人，以"现代诗"在中国新文学界做出了重大贡献。这种风格深受西方文学的影响，在其长达 60 年的职业生涯中，艾青撰写了大量著作，创作了超过 20 首的抒情诗以及 1000 首短诗和近 200 篇涉及广泛主题的散文，从自然叙事主义到政治激进主义，从对中国人民的贫穷和苦难经历的同情到对共产主义事业的欢庆。他一直是一个激进的活动家，后来成为热情的共产主义分子。

Ai Qing, pseudonym of Jiang Haicheng (born on March 27th, 1910, Jinhua, Zhejiang Province, China, died on May 5th, 1996, Beijing), was a renowned poet who made a significant contribution to the new literary genre of "modern poetry" in China. This style, was greatly influenced by western literature. In a career that spanned over 60 years, Ai Qing wrote prolifically, producing over 20 lyrical and narrative poems as well as 1,000 short poems and nearly 200 essays touching upon a broad range of topics from naturalist description to political activism, from empathy towards China's poor and their harsh existence to celebration of the Communist cause. He was always a radical activist and later an ardent communist.

人们对他的诗歌的看法大相径庭：一方面受到广大群众的欢迎，另一方面他也遭到了严厉批判，并作为右派流放了 20 年。一些中国的年轻诗人指责他是一个政治傀儡，阻碍了其他风格的诗歌发展和其他年轻诗人的创作方式，但他也受到了极大的尊敬，就像一位工厂工人曾经写信给他说的那样："我读书不多，但我喜欢你的诗。我明白你说的话。我总是被你的作品感动。"

Opinions about his poetry vary widely: seemingly welcomed by the masses, he was also severely criticized by the establishment and exiled for 20 years as a rightist. Some of China's young poets accused him of being a political puppet and blocking the way for other styles of poetry and younger poets. But he was greatly respected, as one factory worker once wrote to him: "I don't read much. But I like your poems. I understand what you say in them. I am always moved by your works."

据艾青自己回忆，1910 年他出生在浙江一户地主家庭，因为导致他母亲经历了痛苦漫长的难产，他被视为不祥的人。他被送去给别人照料，由一个贫穷的农妇抚养长大，这个农妇不得不把自己的女婴溺死在厕所里才能养育一个富人的儿子。

Born in 1910 in a land owning family in Zhejiang Province, Ai Qing remembered that he would be the bearer of ominous because his mother had undergone a painfully long labour. He was sent away to be nursed, and brought up by a poor peasant woman who had to drown her own infant girl in the toilet in order to bring up a rich person's son.

与农妇一起度过的这五年对他的诗歌产生了巨大的影响,这不仅是因为他的第一首广受赞誉的诗——1933 年《大堰河——我的保姆》,是关于她,也因为他继承了她作为一个贫穷农民对土地的热情。这种热情是如此强烈,也促使他走向了毛泽东投身的革命事业。

The five years Ai Qing stayed with her had a great impact on his poetry, not only because his first widely acclaimed poem, *Dayanhe: My Nurse*, written in 1933, was about her, but also because he inherited from her the passion of a poor peasant for the land. This passion was so intense that it led him to the Maoist revolutionary cause.

日本侵略中国东北促使在巴黎学美术的艾青回家,但在回到上海后,他几乎立即被法国特许警察逮捕,因他参与了左翼艺术家联盟的活动。

Ai Qing was studying art in Paris when Japan's invasion of north-eastern China caused him to return home. But almost immediately after arriving in Shanghai, he was arrested by police in with French concession for involvement in activities of the League of Left-wing Artists.

他三年的牢狱生涯成为他职业生涯中另一个重要转折点:因为他在狱中无法作画,他开始写诗。尽管如此,他对色彩和光线的了解以及捕捉图像的能力对他的写作产生了巨大的影响。

His three years in jail became another important turning-point in his career: he started to write poems because he was unable to paint in prison. Nonetheless his knowledge of colour and light as well as his ability to catch images contributed tremendously to his writing.

正如《雪落在中国的土地上》写道:"风 / 像一个太悲哀了的老妇 / 紧紧地跟随者 / 伸出寒冷的指爪 / 拉扯着行人的衣襟";又如《补衣妇》:"她的孩子哭了 / 眼泪又被太阳晒干了 / 她不知道 / 只是无声地想着她的家 / 她的被炮火毁掉的家……"就是他典型的塑造自然与人文的天赋

表达，与他的政治作品有着明显的对比，如："所有的政策都必须进行的，所有的冤假错案必须纠正／即使是死／必戒。"

He has lines like the following from *the work*: "The Wind / Like a grief-stricken old woman / Closely following behind / Stretching out her ice claws / Tugs at the travellers' clothes"; or from The Women Mending Clothes: "Her baby begins crying / The child's tears dried by the sun / she does not notice it / Silently she thinks of her home/ Its shelter destroyed by gunfire..."are typical of his genius for portraying nature and humanity, and contrast markedly with his more political works such as: "All policies must be carried out, all unjust cases must be righted / Even those who are dead / Must be rehabilitated."

抗日战争期间，爱国主义在中国兴起风暴，受此影响，艾青最终来到延安——共产国际红军革命根据地。他于1941正式加入中国共产党，与毛泽东有过几次接触，毛泽东曾多次与他谈文学政策。1949艾青回到北京时，他已是新政府的干部，开始越来越多地把自己的才能集中在抒写毛泽东和斯大林的赞歌上。

During the Sino-Japanese war, being influenced by rising storm of patriotism in China, Ai Qing eventually travelled to Yan'an, the capital of the Communist-controlled area. He officially joined the Party in 1941, and met Mao Tse-tung several times, who talked to him on several occasions about literary policy. When Ai Qing returned to Beijing in 1949 he was already a cadre in the new government, and began to concentrate his talents more and more on writing poems in praise of Mao Tse-tung and Stalin.

作为一个官方代表他访问了许多国家，直到1958他被公开指责为右派。一篇刊登在官方文学期刊《文学与艺术》的文章说道："……比较奇怪的是，这些文章它们都是反革命的，是由那些似乎具有革命态度的作家们创作出来的。"

He visited many countries as an official delegate until 1958 when he was publicly denounced as a rightist. An article in *Literature and Arts*, an official literary journal, talked about his writing: "...The more peculiar thing about these articles is that they are all counter-revolutionary, but were produced by writers who seemed to has a revolutionary attitude."

随后他先被流放在中国东北,然后又去了西北。他受害的原因仍不清楚,但是,他始终是一个诚挚的毛泽东思想拥护者。从他在返回北京时写的《鱼化石》诗中可以清楚地感受到他受到的苦难:"你绝对的静,对外界毫无反应,看不到天和水,听不见浪花的声音……"

He was subsequently exiled firstly in Northeast China, and then in Northwest. The reasons for his victimization remain unclear, however, as he was always a sincere Maoist. The depth of his suffering can be felt clearly in his poem *Fish Fossil*, written upon his return to Beijing: "So absolutely motionless, you have no reaction to the world. You cannot see the water or the sky, you cannot hear the sound of the waves . . ."

不管人们如何看待艾青的政治立场和他后期写作的政治元素,他的描写力、感情深度和艺术激情都标志着他是一位相当有影响力的诗人。他的作品被他的人生经历,爱恨憎恶打上了不可磨灭的烙印,这些正是人类精神力量的有力表达,同时在中国现代诗歌史上有着十分特殊的地位。

Regardless of how one views Ai Qing's political stance and political aspects of his later writing, his powers of description, depth of feeling and artistic passion mark him out as a poet of considerable presence. His works were indelibly marked by the period of turmoil in which he lived, worked, loved, hated and survived, and as such are powerful expressions of human spirit and hold a special place in modern Chinese poetry.

注释:
① Source: http://www.tlfjw.com/xuefo-232252.html 中文有修改。
② Source: https://en.wikipedia.org/wiki/Luo_Binwang 英文有修改。
③ Source: http://www.en8848.com.cn/read/sybk/lsmr/294472.html
④ Source: http://www.kekenet.com/read/201604/435073.shtml

⑤ Source: https://en.wikipedia.org/wiki/Li_Yu_(author) 英文有修改。

⑥ Source:Wikipedia:https://en.wikipedia.org/wiki/Huang_Binhong

第四章　民间艺术

Chapter Four Folk Arts

第一节　民间表演 Folk Performances

婺剧[①]　Wu Opera

婺剧，浙江省地方戏曲剧种之一。它以金华地区为中心，流行于金华、丽水、临海、建德、淳安以江西东北部的玉山、上饶、贵溪、波阳、景德镇等地，是高腔、昆曲、乱弹、徽戏、滩簧、时调六种声腔的合班。俗称"金华戏"，因金华古称婺州，1949 年改今称。

Wu Opera, one kind of local operas in Zhejiang Province, centered in Jinhua, is popular in places such as Jinhua, Lishui, Linhai, Jiande, Chun'an and northeast parts of Jiangxi province like Yushan, Shangrao, Guixi, Boyang, Jingdezhen, etc. It is combination of six famous Opera Tune Patterns, that is, Gaoqiang Tune, Kun Opera, Luantan Tune, Hui Opera, Tanhuang Tune and Shidiao Tune. Traditionally, it is named Jinhua Opera, and for the reason that Jinhua is called Wuzhou in ancient times, so here came the name Wu Opera from the year 1949.

高腔有侯阳、西吴、西安、松阳之分。侯阳高腔流行于东阳、义乌一带，有人认为可能是义乌腔的派生，擅演武戏。西吴高腔因在金华北乡的西吴村开设科班而得名,其唱腔较西安高腔委婉、质朴,且多滚唱,与徽池雅调有渊源关系。西安高腔流行于衢州一带,衢州古称"西安",故名。相传与弋阳腔有密切关系,也有人认为可能是西平腔的遗响。其曲调字多腔少,具有一泄而尽的特点。以上三种,均一人启唱,众人帮腔,锣鼓助节,音调随心入腔。

Gaoqiang Tune can be divided into Houyang, Xiwu, Xi'an and Songyang. The Houyang Gaoqiang Tune which is good at playing martial play, is popular in Dongyang and Yiwu region. Some people think Gaoqiang may derive from Yiwu accent. Xiwu Gaogiang Tune tune got its name for it once started opera training schools in Xiwu village in northern part of Jinhua. Its tune is much softer and plainer than the Xi'an Gaoqiang Tune and it is said to have something to do with the Huichiya tune. The Xi'an Gaoqiang Tune is so called because Quzhou was once named Xi'an in ancient times and it has been popular in Quzhou since then. According to legend, it is closely related to the Yiyang Tune or some may believe it evolved from the Xiping Tune. It is characterized by more lyrics but less melody.The above three tunes all have one person leading the tune and other people echoing with gong and drum to help the section, thus making the tune deep into heart.

昆曲,俗称"草昆""金昆",是昆腔流传在金华一带的支派。因长期流动演出于农村的草台和庙会,以农民为主要观众对象,故语言较通俗,追求情节曲折,唱腔也不拘泥于四声格腔,以演武戏、做工戏、大戏为主。在明代之后,一直被视为婺剧诸声腔中的正宗。实际上是昆曲在衢州(今衢江区一带)、金华的一个支流,在语言、曲调上均结合当地习惯予以简化或改变,故称"草昆"。

Kun Opera, commonly known as "Caokun" or "Jinkun" , is one of the branches spreading in Jinhua and its vicinity. It is performed on grass platform and at temple fair in rural areas, with farmers as the main target audience. Therefore, its language is much popular, the plot is complicated and intricate, its aria doesn't rigidly adhere to the four-tone pattern, and performers mainly show the traditional martial arts and show a full-scale traditional opera. After the Ming Dynasty, it was regarded as the orthodox Jinhua Opera among numerous tunes. Actually Kunqu Opera is a branch in Quzhou (present Qu County area) and Jinhua. As it has been simplified and changed by combining its language and tune with the local customs, it is called "Caokun" today.

乱弹，因专工乱弹的"乱弹班"多出自浦江县，故又称"浦江乱弹"。以二凡、三五七、芦花为主要唱调。其流行地区除金华、衢州、严州（治今浙江建德）外，也常在昌化、桐庐一带演出。二凡具北方戏曲唱腔的特点，有人认为其源于西秦腔，也有人认为源于安徽的吹腔和四平调。

Luantan Tune is also called "Pujiang Luantan" as most of the specialized Luantan troupes come from Pujiang. Its main tune is Erfan, Sanwuqi (Three, Five, Seven) and Luhua. It is popular not only in Jinhua, Quzhou and Yanzhou (present Jiande, Zhejiang), but also in Changhua and Tonglu. Erfan shares the same characteristics with operas in northern China. Some believe that it originatesd from the tune of West Qin, some others believe that it comes from Chuiqiang and Siping Tune in Anhui.

徽戏，自皖南传入。清末以来，大量皖人迁往金华一带，多数经商，徽戏随商路流入，金华、衢州两府本地徽班达三十余个，仅1918年前后开设的本地科班就有十余个。婺剧徽班自成一格，以拔子、芦花、吹腔等老徽调为主。唱西皮、二黄，表演粗犷、泼赖、朴实、健康。

Hui Opera was brought by people from south Anhui Province. During the late Qing Dynasty, numerous people in Anhui moved to Jinhua and its surroundings, most of whom did business. Thus Anhui Opera came here. The local Anhui Opera troupes in Jinhua and Quzhou amount to over thirty, and over ten local training schools just set up around 1918. The Anhui troupes of Wu Opera have their unique style, characterized by the ancient tune of Anhui Opera like Bazi, Luhua, and Chuiqiang, etc. They sing Xipi and Erhuang and give a straightforward, bold, plain and healthy performance.

滩簧,相传源出苏州滩簧。乾隆、嘉庆年间,金华已有曲艺滩簧坐唱班。有人认为,滩簧系由往来于衢州、兰江的花船船嬢卖艺带入,先有业余坐唱班,后由婺剧艺人衍为戏曲,成为婺剧声腔之一。有"浦江滩簧""兰溪滩簧""东阳滩簧"之分。剧目有《僧尼会》《断桥》《牡丹对课》等。

Tanhuang Tune, according to legend, originated from Suzhou Tanhuang. During the reign of Emperor Qianlong and Jiaqing in the Qing Dynasty , there was Tanhuang choir in Jinhua. Some believe that Tanhuang Tune was brought here by the female performers on the boats between Quzhou and Lanjiang River. At the beginning it was just amateur choir, and then it developed into an opera by Wu Opera performers, being a tune of Wu Opera. It can be divided into Pujiang Tanhuang, Lanxi Tanhuang and Dongyang Tanhuang, with a list of plays like *Sengnihui*, *Duanqiao*, *Mudanduike*, and so on.

时调,是明清以来时尚民间小戏的统称。有的来自明清俗曲,有的属南罗,有的为油滩,有的源于地方小调。由当地民歌、歌舞演变而成,是一种演唱农村生活小戏的声腔,剧目有《走广东》《卖棉纱》《王婆骂鸡》等。

Shidiao Tune is a general term referring to the popular tunes in a particular locality during the Ming and Qing Dynasties, some originate from common folk songs of Ming and Qing Dynasties, some belong to Nanluo, some from Youtan, and some from local tunes. Evolved from local folk songs and dances, it is a kind of tune showing the country life, with a list of plays like *Zouguangdong* , *Maimiansha* , *Wangpomaji* , and so on.

以上六种声腔,在婺剧中不是一戏混用,而是各个声腔都有一批专长剧目。最初,高腔、昆腔、乱弹等独立成班,后发展为合班,并有不同的组合。高、昆、乱兼唱的戏班,俗称"三合班"。以后,徽戏传入金华一带,有的三合班弃高腔而兼唱徽戏,有的徽班却兼唱乱弹。之后,又吸收了滩簧和时调。

The above six tunes are not used in confusion in Wu Opera. Instead, every single tune has its special list of plays. At first, the Gopqiang Tune tune, Kun opera tune and Luantan tune give performance in their respective troupe, and then they develop into a joint troupe, with different combinations. A theatrical troupe, with the high-pitched tune, Kun opera tune and Luantan tune performing concurrently, is called "tri-joint troupe". After Anhui Opera came to Jinhua, some tri-joint troupes give up Gao melody and perform Anhui Opera concurrently, and some Anhui Opera troupes perform Luantan tune concurrently. Later, Tanhuang tune and Shidiao tune are also adopted.

婺剧的传统剧目有《断桥》《对课》《僧尼会》，其中《断桥》被周恩来赞为"天下第一桥"。它吸收了高腔、昆曲、乱弹、徽戏、滩簧、时调六种声腔。当代，涌现出郑兰香、吴光耀、陈美兰、张建敏等一批著名的婺剧表演艺术家。2008年婺剧入选第二批国家级非物质文化遗产名录。在2016年，婺剧同时上了新年戏曲晚会和春节晚会。

The traditional shows of Wu Opera include *Broken Bridge*, *The Eloquence of Miss Peony* and *The Encounter of a Monk and a Nun*, in which *Broken Bridge* was admired as "the First Bridge in the World" by Premier Zhou Enlai. It has absorbed six tunes, namely Gopqiang Tune, Kun Opera, Luantan Tune, Hui Opera, Tanhuang Tune and Shidiao Tune. A group of famous contemporary performers of Wu Opera has emerged, such as Zheng Lanxiang, Wu Guangyao, Chen Meilan, Zhang Jianmin, etc. It was listed among the second batch of National Intangible Cultural Relics in 2008. It was on the performing lists of New Year Opera Gala and Spring Festival Gala in 2016.

婺剧脸谱是在"古老彩绘图腾"的基础上形成和发展的。一般讲脸谱，总是指大花和小花，而婺剧则除此以外，还有四花、小生、老生、老外、副末，甚至连个别花旦、作旦、武旦等角色也有脸谱。婺剧脸谱颜色代表性格，图案也有寓意。

Wu Opera masks were originated and developed from "the ancient painted totem". Generally speaking, masks refer to facial paintings of Da Hua Lian (Jing, persons with unique features) and Xiao Hua Lian (Chou, clown), but apart from these two, Wu Opera has other masks for different roles, such as Sihua, Xiaosheng, Laosheng, Laowai, Fumo, even some particular roles like Huadan, Zuodan and Wudan have their own masks. The color of masks stands for personalities, with patterns for special meanings.

浦江板凳龙　Bench Dragon of Pujiang

据浦江白马镇夏张村张姓族谱载,自唐朝始,"龙腾灯舞闹元宵"便成了浦江民间的习俗,浦江县志中称之为"灯节"。浦江板凳龙盛行于浦江县乡村,广泛流传于江南沿海各地。综观浦江板凳龙的传承发展,唐代为其孕育期,宋、元为其成熟期,明、清为其鼎盛期。

According to the family tree of Zhang, in Xiazhang, Baima Town, Pujiang County. There are some kinds of dragon dances, among which the bench dragon is the most popular among local people. It is also called as "Lantern Festival". Dragon dance had been a custom of Lantern Festival in Tang, developed into its mature period in Song and Yuan, and the peak period in Ming and Qing.

相传,在很久很久以前,当地遇上了史无前例的干旱,到了井枯、河干的程度,大地一片干枯,渴死的人不计其数,人们祈求天上能下场大雨,可不管怎样,雨总是下不来。这事被东海的一条水龙看在眼里,看到万物枯死,生灵干死,它不顾一切跃出水面,在当地下了一场大雨,万物复苏,人们得到了解救,可水龙由于违反了天规,被剁成一段一段,撒向人间。人们忍着悲痛,把龙体放在板凳上,并把它连接起来(后来,直至现在,人们称之为"板凳龙")。人们不分昼夜地奔走相告,希望它能活下来,舞"板凳龙"的习俗也由此产生了。

Long time ago, Pujiang suffered a terrible drou which was unprecedented. As subsequent consequence, countless people died of lacking water. Local people prayed for rain again and again, but it did not work. Until a dragon of East Sea, who was a god being able to generate rain under the Yuhuang God's order, opened his mind to those dying people, so that he made rain for them regardless of the ban of the Yuhuang God. Because of the rain, people were saved, while the dragon had to face the punishment of being chopped into pieces and being thrown down to the world of mortals. Local people thanked for his help and collected all pieces of his body, putting them on the benches and connecting them one by one. They hoped that the dragon would relive in that way. Thereupon, the bench dragon dance came into being.

浦江板凳龙，顾名思义就是一条条用单个板凳串联而成的游动的龙灯。从构造上看，浦江板凳龙由龙头、龙身（子灯）、龙尾三部分组成。

As implied by the name, Pujiang bench dragon is the dragon-like lanterns consisting of benches. It has dragon head, dragon body and dragon tail.

龙头其实由两部分组成，核心部分是木雕的一条小型的完整的龙，有些甚至是用黄金打造。平时这条龙贡奉在每个村的祠堂，而到元宵节期间，正月十一，这条龙就会被抬到堂头，人们在上过香后，会有专门的人为它套上一个竹篾扎成的巨型龙头。龙头下托木板，高 2 米，长 4 米，外面裱上棉纸，再绘上色彩鲜艳的龙鳞，而龙头造型不一，有缄口与张口之分，胡须有白、黑之别。白胡须灯头称为老灯头，张口翘舌黑胡须灯头，表示年轻。而每当一个龙头装饰完毕之后，会有一个挂彩的仪式，即把不同颜色的布匹披在龙头上。人们把自己买的布匹披上龙头，祈求龙能够在新的一年保佑全家人。此外，还会让幼童从龙头下面钻过去，同样是为了祈福。元宵夜会演，黑胡须灯头提早进场先行串演，白胡须灯头入场后，它同时陪迎三圈结束时黑胡须灯头提前退场，谓年轻礼让年长之仪。

The head has two parts in fact. The essence of the head is a complete wood carved dragon. Sometimes it is made from gold. Ordinarily it is enshrined and worshiped by villagers in the ancestral shrine. During the Lantern Festival, since 11th day of lunar January, the dragon will be placed at Tangtou, enjoying incense. Then they will put it into a huge dragon head with bamboo outline pasted over by cotton paper, which is 2 meters high, 4 meters long. On the paper, colorful scales are painted. The heads have different shapes, some of them open their mouths, some of them close, some of them wear white beard, and some of them have black sideburns. Black means they are junior, while the white are senior. When the head is painted well, it will be decorated with colored silk festoons as well. People drape the festoons over the head to pray for happiness for the whole family. Besides, children are asked to walk through under the head, because the dragon will bless the children in that way. In the meeting, the black one will dance first and then welcome the white ones. When the program is over, the black ones also draw back first to show their respect to the older.

通常龙所到的大村都要盘龙。选择能容纳整条龙盘旋的场地（多为晒谷场），无场地的选面积较大的田块。被龙踩过的田块当年会获得大丰收。板凳龙每年都要到附近同姓的村子串演，龙虎旗、云锣开道，所到之处均以火炮、香烛迎送。除了到各村的祠堂、厅堂祭拜外，一些户家为求平安、求发财、求子也将龙头请到自家门前祭拜，并送以红包、馒头。求子的还要在龙头上摘一小球挂于床前，一旦求子求成，一般在第二年还要来分馒头致谢。

Dragon will coil up on the playground, or on the field. It is said after being stepped by the dragon, the field will generate more grain output. To welcome the dragon, fervent people will set off firecrackers and offer the incense. The rich also will plead the dragon to pass their house to pray for peace, wealth and sons. After that, the rich will present lucky money and steamed buns. Some women will hang little balls of the dragon head over their beds with a hope of having a son. If their hope comes true, they will thank the dragon next year.

舞龙中最具看头的就是盘龙。盘龙一旦开始，鞭炮鼓乐齐鸣，龙头领先，龙身龙尾相随，呈圆形盘旋。盘旋的圈数一般为顺时针三圈、逆时针三圈。盘旋的速度随着鼓乐由缓到急。人们举着板凳，模仿着龙舞动时的姿态盘旋着。龙身越盘越紧，舞龙者的脚步也越来越快，到最后几乎是在狂奔了。

The most worth watching scene is the dragon coiling itself in the dragon dance. In the jubilant voice of gong, drumts, and firecrackers, the head leads the whole dragon to coil up round and round. Due to the centrifugal force, the dragon becomes tighter and tighter. And the holders have to run faster and faster to avoid being flung.

一条浦江板凳龙几乎就是一个艺术综合体,它集书法、绘画、剪纸、刻花、雕塑艺术和扎制编糊工艺为一体,融体育、杂技、舞蹈为一炉。游动起来的龙舞兼有粗犷、细腻、奔放、严整的风格,通过这种激情与哲理、娱乐教化合一的舞蹈,人们得到了感官和心灵的双重满足。浦江板凳龙是地道的百姓文化,广场性、广泛性、惊险性为其主要特征,其参加人数之多、活动场地之大,在同类形式中实属罕见。

A bench dragon is a perfect complex of penmanship, painting, paper-cut, carving and bamboo craft, a wonderful complex of sport, dance, acrobatics. When it begins to dance, it shows the beauty of passion as well as philosophy. It is bold and unconstrained, but it is fine and delicate too. It pleases people physically and mentally. As a native people culture, it has incompatible scale in terms of the number of participants and the size of site.

金华斗牛 Jinhua Bullfight

金华素有二绝之说,一是火腿,二是斗牛。金华斗牛,民风古朴,源远流长,但金华斗牛风俗究竟始于何时已无法考证。据清末进士、县人王廷扬所作《斗牛歌》小序中云:金华斗牛"始于赵宋明道年间(1032—1033)",积习相沿,经久不衰,是带有东方文明独特魅力的汉族民俗游乐活动,其风情可与西班牙斗牛相媲美,被称为"东方一绝"。

There are two uniques, one is Jinhua ham, the other is bullfight. Jinhua bullfight has a long history among simple folks. However, there is no record telling about its origin. According to *The Chant to Bullfighting* written by Wang Tingyang—a Jinshi in the late Qing Dynasty, it is said that Jinhua bullfight started from the Mingdao period of the Song Dynasty (1032—

1033) and has passed down till now. It is a folk entertainment, featuring Eastern civilization. Jinhua bullfight comparing favourably with the Spanish Bullfighting is renowned as "The Eastern Unique Skill".

金华斗牛，至今已有千年历史，清末民初尤其盛行。金华斗牛是牛与牛斗，不同于西班牙的人与牛斗。在金华斗牛中，不会对牛有伤害。斗牛时，参斗之牛成对被送入斗牛场，

Jinhua bullfight with a history of about 1,000 years was especially popular in late Qing and the early Republic of China. Being different from Spanish bullfight, Jinhua bullfight is about bull-to-bull fight but not man-to-bull fight, and no harm is done to the bulls in Jinhua's tradition.

斗牛时日，一般选定在春秋农闲之际，数十天便举行一次，多选周山环抱的水田为场地。斗牛当日，参斗之牛佩以勇士之饰，由其主人护送进入斗牛场，此时传统乐队（使用中国传统乐器）开始演奏。斗牛结束后，参斗之牛再次由主人带回农田从事农作。

The bullfight day is usually set at farmers' leisure time in Autumn or Spring, and the bullfight is often held at paddy fields surrounded by mountains every dozen of days. On the Day, the bulls wearing warrior ornaments are escorted by the owners to the bullring, and at the same time, the bands of musicians accompany the event on a variety of traditional Chinese instruments, and when it's all over the owners take the bulls back to the farms where they are used in agriculture.

第二节 工艺美术 Arts and Crafts

东阳木雕 Dongyang Woodcarving

木雕是中国传统民间工艺，最早可追溯到新石器时代。木雕工艺历史悠久源远流长，中国目前有四大木雕：乐清黄杨木雕、东阳木雕、广东潮州木雕和福建龙眼木雕。东阳木雕作为四大木雕之一，中华民族最优秀

的民间工艺之一，被誉为"国之瑰宝"。

Woodcarving is a traditional folk handicraft in China. Its origin can be traced back to the New Stone Age. With a long history, the handicraft has developed into four major schools: Yueqing Huangyang Woodcarving, Dongyang Woodcarving, Guangdong Chaozhou Woodcarving and Fujian Longyan Woodcarving. As one of the four major schools of woodcarving, Dongyang Woodcarving has been reputed as one of the best folk handicrafts and a national treasure.

东阳自古以来被誉为木雕之乡。最早出现于唐朝，精湛于宋朝。在明清时期，东阳木雕发展迅速，欣欣向荣，也在那时，东阳成为全国木雕生产基地。创作出了大量的木雕作品，比如佛像和用于宫殿、寺庙、园林和民宿的装饰性建筑构件。清乾隆年间，东阳木雕享誉全国。约四百名东阳木匠被招募入京修复皇室宫殿。其中有些木匠为皇室打造木制家具。辛亥革命之后，东阳木雕逐渐商业化。众多木雕作品销往香港、美国和东南亚，木雕工厂也如雨后春笋般出现。1914年在杭州成立的仁艺厂是最早的东阳木雕厂。在抗日战争和内战时期，东阳木雕逐渐萧条。中华人民共和国成立后，政府召集和组织了木雕工，建立了合作社。到目前为止，东阳木雕已经拥有七大类的3600多个木雕种类。其中包括木雕屏风，挂屏以及新款插屏、随着时代的发展，东阳木雕不断改进，坚持创新，正以最好的姿态走向更加美好的明天。

Dongyang has been honored as the hometown of woodcarving since ancient times. Dongyang Woodcarving came into being early in Tang Dynasty. In Song Dynasty, it reached a high state of art. During the period of Ming Dynasty and Qing Dynasty, Dongyang Woodcarving came into flourishing. At that time, Dongyang gradually became the national base of woodcarving. It produced a great amount of woodcarvings including Buddha sculptures and ornamental architectural components designed for palaces, temples, gardens and folk houses. During the reign of Emperor Qianlong in Qing Dynasty, Dongyang Woodcarving spread its name to every corner of China. About 400 skillful Dongyang woodcarvers were recruited to the capital to restore the palaces. Some of them went to the court to make wood furniture for the emperor. After Xinhai Revolution, namely the 1911 Revolution, Dongyang Woodcarving was gradually commercialized. Many woodcarvings were sold to Hong Kong, the US and the Southeast Asia. And factories of Dongyang Woodcarving sprung up one after another. Renyi Factory, established in 1914 in Hangzhou, was the first Dongyang Woodcarving factory. But later during the War of Resistance Against Japan and the civil war, Dongyang Woodcarving suffered severe depression. After the establishment of PRC, the dispersed carvers were organized by the government and a cooperative was set up. Now, Dongyang Woodcarving has developed 7 major categories covering more than 3600 varieties of Dongyang Woodcarving. Among them, carved wooden folding screens, hanging screens and table screens are new styles of Dongyang woodcarving. As time goes on, Dongyang Woodcarving is stepping towards a bright future by continuous innovation and improvement.

竹编 Bamboo Weaving

东阳竹编历史悠久，名师辈出，工艺精巧，风格独特，同"东阳木雕"一起堪称盛开在东阳江畔的一对民间工艺艺术姊妹花，是中国传统工艺美术园地中的一个很有特色的品种。

Dongyang has a long history in weaving bamboo articles. There emerged generations of famous craftsmen with exquisite craftsmanship and unique style. Dongyang Bamboo Weaving with its twin Dongyang Wood Carving is quite distinctive folk art in China's traditional art.

竹编工艺起源于原始社会。东阳竹编在殷商时代问世。东阳竹编的元宵花灯、龙灯和走马灯之类竹编工艺灯，在宋代已闻名四方。明清时期，竹编技艺发展迅速，竹编工艺品的艺术性与实用性进一步紧密结合，上至送往京城皇亲国戚的"贡品"，下到寻常百姓的家常生活用品，比比皆是。清代康熙年间的竹编工艺，主要生产门帘、果盒、托篮等产品，其中书箱、香篮还广泛流行于绍兴、诸暨、嵊州、新昌一带。

Bamboo weaving originated from the primitive society. Dongyang Bamboo weaving came into being since Yin and Shang Dynasties. The lanterns, dragon lanterns and shadow-picture lanterns made of bamboos in Dongyang won a nationwide popularity in Song Dynasty. In the Ming and Qing Dynasties, the bamboo-weaving craftsmanship developed fast and got a further integration with utility and artistry. The qualified products as tributes were not only sent to the court but also sold to the folks. In the Kangxi Period of the Qing Dynasty, the bamboo-woven products mainly included door curtains, fruit containers and baskets. Particularly, bookcases and incense-baskets were widely popular in Shaoxing, Zhuji, Shengzhou and Xinchang.

东阳竹编实用产品有篮、盘、包、箱、瓶、罐、家具等 20 多种,动物竹编产品有鸡、鸭、鹅、兔、狗等,形象夸张生动。

There are more than twenty categories--basket plate, bag, case, bottle, can and furniture-among Dongyang bamboo-weaving practical articles, and there are bamboo-weaving images such as chicken, duck, goose, rabbit and dog, exaggerated but vivid.

经历代东阳竹编艺人的努力,竹编工艺还突破传统理念的束缚,巧妙地与园林建筑、室内装饰有机结合起来,在西湖阮公墩、杭州花港公园、德国汉堡市新北京酒家等处,留下了许多不朽佳作。

With efforts made by bamboo-weaving craftsmen of Dongyang, they have broken through the constraint of traditional concepts and have made a combination with garden building and indoor decoration skilfully. There are many great masterpieces at Ruangong Mound of West Lake, Huagang Park of Hangzhou, New Beijing Restaurant at Hamburg, Germany.

剪纸 Paper Cutting

浦江剪纸历史悠久,据传南宋时期就已相当盛行,是浙江省汉族传统手工艺品,明清时已在农村广泛流传,现在尚能见到一些清末民初的作品。

The historical Pujiang Paper Cutting prevailing in the Southern Song Dynasty is a traditional handicraft of Han people in Zhejiang Province. Works of paper cutting widely spread in rural places during the Ming-Qing Dynasties when a certain amount of these works were created can still be traced.

浦江剪纸风格秀丽,装饰性强,并极具想象力,题材广泛,以花鸟动物和戏剧人物居多。花鸟动物多以祈求吉祥如意、多子多福、荣禄富贵为主题。浦江剪纸中的动物形象栩栩如生,动感十足。浦江剪纸尤以戏曲窗花为最佳,多数作品有着规整的外框。浦江剪纸工艺精巧、题材广泛,生活情趣浓郁,尤其是清代地方戏曲。浦江剪纸采用戏曲人物作为题材成为一种尝试和追求。浦江戏曲人物剪纸在浦江乱弹的独特艺术效应下生发灵性,逐步发展成一种风格独特的剪纸艺术类型,从而成为中国剪纸主要流派之一。

Pujiang Paper Cutting, which features beautiful style, strong decoration and rich imagination, has a broad range of subjects from animals, flowers and birds to opera figures. These works to a larger extent are themed by best wishes for good fortune, household fertility, wealth and honor. The animals of paper cutting are true to life, with a dynamic and metrical presentation of images. Being inclined to themes of opera, Pujiang Paper Cutting is framed in order. It features in exquisite craftsmanship, extensive subjects and joy of life. In particular, the subjects and images of regional operas of Qing Dynasty is a brand new attempt and creation. Under the influence and inspiration of the distinctive art of Pujiang Luantan, Pujiang Paper Cutting has being gradually developed into a uniquely styled branch of Chinese Paper Cutting.

2008年入选第一批国家级非物质文化遗产扩展项目名录。

Pujiang Paper Cutting was enrolled in the first batch of National Intangible Cultural Heritage Expansion Project Directory in 2008.

婺州窑　WuZhou Kiln

唐以后,金华称婺州,因兰溪、义乌、东阳、永康、武义、衢州、江山等地区烧制的瓷器在胎、釉、造型以及装饰风格上有共同特征而统称婺州窑。浙江是中国成熟瓷器的发源地,而婺州窑又是浙江青瓷的代表作之一,自汉代到明朝1800多年间走过了漫长历程。它在西汉时开始出现,东汉中晚期烧制出真正意义上的成熟婺州窑瓷器,在六朝时得到较大发展,到唐宋时期趋于鼎盛,是唐代六大青瓷产区之一。

Since Tang Dynasty, Jinhua has been called Wuzhou. So Wuzhou Porcelains refer to the porcelains which are made in Jinhua and its nearby districts including Lanxi, Yiwu, Dongyang, Yongkang, Wuyi, Quzhou and Jiangshan, with similar style in body, glaze and modeling. Zhejiang Province is an original place of mature porcelains in China, and Wuzhou porcelains is one of the representatives of Zhejiang celadon porcelains with a long history of 1800 years from Han Dynasty to Ming Dynasty. Wuzhou District was one of the six producing regions of celadon porcelains in Tang Dynasty. They originally appeared in Western Han Dynasty, became mature in the true sense in the middle and late Eastern Han Dynasty, and got extensive development in the Six Dynasties and reached their peak in the Tang and Song Dynasties.

到目前为止,金华已发掘出古代窑址六百多处,数量之多,生产年代之长,在我国瓷器生产史上均属罕见。婺州窑烧制的主要是民用瓷,大量生产人们日常生活用的碗、盆、罐、壶等以及一些民器,和人民生活的关系非常紧密。

It is quite rare that more than 600 ancient kilns have been unearthed in Jinhua, covering a large range of years in Jinhua. Wuzhou porcelains are mainly for civil use, producing a great number of bowls, basins and pots which were daily used by people and were closely related with people's life.

婺州窑具有较高价值,中国工艺美术馆馆长、中国艺术研究院博士生导师吕品田先生这样评价婺州窑:婺州窑持续历史很长,作为民间窑场,在中国陶瓷史上占有很高的地位。

Wuzhou porcelains are highly valued. Mr. Lv Pintian, curator of China Arts and Crafts Museum and supervisor of PHD students in China Academy of Arts, evaluated that Wuzhou Kiln has a long history and as a folk kiln, enjoys a high position in the history of Chinese porcelains.

婺州窑是唐代制瓷名窑。金衢盆地发现的婺州窑遗址多达600多处，窑址一般依水而建，一是烧窑取水方便，二是运输靠水运。宋以前的婺州窑以龙窑为主，龙窑又分为分室龙窑与统间龙窑（分室龙窑是统间龙窑的改进版，将窑室进行分隔，使其受热均匀，成品率更高），南宋以后馒头窑随着北方文化传入金华。统间龙窑一般建在有坡度的丘陵上，在窑址旁边人们会把烧坏的瓷器扔到山脚下，逐渐堆积形成了一个堆积层，越下面的年代越久远。窑身两边有一些小孔，这些小孔就是投柴孔，一般烧瓷都会用松木来做燃料，因为松木热量高，火焰长，灰粉质少。

In Tang Dynasty, Wuzhou Kiln was quite famous for making porcelains. By now, more than 600 Wuzhou kilns were found Jinhua - Quzhou Basin. Generally, the kilns were constructed near water flows for two reasons. Firstly, it was easy to fetch water for making porcelains. Secondly, it was convenient to transport porcelains by waterway. Before the Song Dynasty, most Wuzhou kilns were Dragon kilns. Normally, there are two different kinds of Dragon Kiln, Loculatous Dragon Kiln and All-in-one Dragon Kiln (Loculatous Dragon Kiln was the improvement from All-in-one Dragon Kiln and the chamber was separated so that it would be heated evenly and higher rate of finished products could be attained). Since the South Song Dynasty, Mantou Kiln had transferred to Jinhua along with the northern culture. Most of them were built on a hill with a slope. Near the kilns, people would throw the failed porcelains to the foot of the mountain. As time went by, more and more porcelains were piled up and the ones stayed at the bottom were the oldest. There are small holes on both sides of the kiln. Actually, they were used as firewood. Pines were widely used for making porcelains because it has good ability in heating and it has a long flame but little ash powder.

它分为窑头、窑床、窑尾三部分。窑头有狭长的火门，火门下是通风口，从这里向火膛进风，使燃料充分燃烧。从横断面积来看窑头最小，窑头头部圆,便于烧窑开始时热量集中。在烧制前,窑工会做一些祭祀活动,以祈祷烧制的顺利。一般在龙窑附近都能发现窑址自然堆积的瓷片层,窑工在烧窑时候把一些残次品和破碎的瓷片随手丢在旁边,越往下年代越早。现在很多婺州窑都有瓷片层的遗址。龙窑作业时,在窑室内码装坯体后,将所有窑门封闭。先烧窑头,由前向后依次投柴,逐排烧成。龙窑的最大优点是升温快,降温也快,可以快烧,也可以维持烧造青瓷的还原焰。

All-in-one Kiln was divided into three parts-the head, the bed and the end. The kiln head had a long but narrow fire gate, under the fire gate, the air flows to the fire chamber, which would make the burning more sufficient. From the cross section, we can know that the kiln head is the smallest part. The kiln head is round so that the heating could be concentrated at the beginning. Before making porcelains, the workers would do some sacrificial activities, hoping the porcelain making could progress barrier-free. In fact, it is quite easy to find some porcelain pieces piled up around the kilns. Porcelain pieces were the defective porcelains and broken ones were thrown away. The ones located at the bottom are normally the oldest. Now, many ruins with porcelain pieces made in the Wuzhou Kiln had been found. When the dragon kiln was to make porcelains, rough bodies were put in the chamber and all the doors should be shut. Kiln head should be heated first, and firewood should be added in sequence from the front to the back. The biggest advantage of the Dragon Kiln is that the temperature rise can be fast, as well as the cooling down, where the porcelain could be made fast and the reducing flame required by celadon could be maintained.

那些窑壁上黑色的结晶体被形象地称为窑汗,这是硅酸盐在一定温度下的结晶。这里面还放有火照,一般窑工在烧窑过程中会用铁丝将火照拿出,检验瓷器是否烧熟。

There are many black crystals which were named as kiln sweat. Actually, at a certain temperature, silicate will be crystallized. In the kiln, test blocks shall be put in. When making the porcelain, the workers would take out the test block by an iron thread to see that whether the porcelain was heated thoroughly enough.

由于龙窑从头到尾有较大的高度差，因而具有一定的自然抽力，本身就起着烟囱的作用，所以窑尾可以不设烟囱。

There is a big height difference between kiln head and kiln end, resulting in a natural draft. So the height difference could be used as a chimney, so there is no need to have a chimney at the kiln end.

注释：

① Source: https://baike.baidu.com/item/%E5%A4%AA%E5%B9%B3%E5%A4%A9%E5%9B%BD%E4%BE%8D%E7%8E%8B%E5%BA%9C/3818625?fr=aladdin

第五章　婺商

Chapter Five Wu Commerce

第一节　经济概况　Profile of Economy

金华的地形以盆地和山地丘陵为主,主要土壤类型有水稻土、红壤、黄壤、潮土、紫色土、石灰岩土。其中红壤、黄壤等酸性土壤占比较大。红壤面积 39.93 万公顷,约占全市土地面积的 1/3,永康、东阳、义乌尤为突出,占了将近一半左右。红土地的特点是酸、瘦、黏,不适合种植粮食作物,制约农业经济发展。

Jinhua's terrain is dominated by basins, mountains and hills. The main soil types are paddy soil, red soil, yellow soil, fluvo-aquic soil, purple soil and limestone soil. Among them, red soil, yellow soil and other acidic soil account for a larger proportion. The area of red soil is 399,300 hectares, accounting for about 1/3 of the city's land area. Red soil in Yongkang, Dongyang and Yiwu occupies nearly half of the land area. Red soil is characterized by acid, barren and sticky, which is not suitable for planting food crops, restricting the development of agricultural economy.

金华汤溪一带流传一首民谣:"红黄泥/红黄泥/晴天刀戳不进/雨天像蜡烛油/只长个癞痢头"这个"癞痢头"说的是马尾松,马尾松是一种荒山造林的树种,对土壤要求不高,在红壤上,马尾松依然也只能稀疏生长。

There is a ballad spreading in Tangxi of Jinhua: red and yellow mud, red and yellow mud, the soil is so hard that knife cannot stab into it in sunny days, while it flows like candle oil in rainy days. Only *Pinus massoniana* can grow in it. *Pinus massoniana* is a tree species in afforestation, which does not need fertile soil and can only grow thinly in the red soil.

到了唐宋,金华人口增长的趋势逐渐明显。根据各县志记载,金华历史上曾出现几次人口增长高峰。唐贞观十四年和唐天宝十一年金华人口的年平均增长率分别为 27% 、14% 以上。到了元明清,人口持续增长。为满足越来越多人口的需要,人们开拓河谷平原和丘陵山地,兴修水利,金华土地保肥性和保湿性不佳,各地利用鸡毛、头发、淘米水、石膏粉等作为肥料促进作物生长,并兴修水利。陂塘是农田主要的灌溉模式。金华还引进了适应红壤生长的茶叶、棉花、甘蔗,还有耐旱早熟的早熟稻。然而,受土壤性质制约,金华人地关系依旧紧张。

In the Tang and Song Dynasties, the trend of population growth in Jinhua gradually became apparent. According to records of the counties, there were several population growth peaks in the history of Jinhua. The annual average growth rate was 27% and 14% above in Zhenguan 14th year and Tianbao 11th year in the Tang Dynasty，respectively. In the Yuan, Ming and Qing Dynasties, the population continued to grow. In order to meet the needs of growing population, people reclaimed valleys, plains, hills and mountains, and built water conservancy projects. The land in Jinhua has poor nutrient preserving capability and poor moisture retention. People used chicken feathers, hair, water from washing rice and gypsum powder as fertilizer to promote crop growth, and built water conservancy projects. The pond was the main irrigation pattern for the farmland. Jinhua also introduced tea, cotton, sugar cane as well as drought-resistant early maturing rice, which adapt to red soil. However, under the restriction of soil properties, the relationship between people and land in Jinhua is still strained.

　　金华人开始寻求新的生存之道。很多人通过耕读求仕谋生，一些大家族从族产资助族中子弟求学，但是能够从仕的一般占少数。南宋以来，婺学盛行，吕祖谦提倡的现实主义，重视工商"商藉农而立，农赖商而行，求以相补，而非求相病"。陈亮也提出利益合一，农商并举，在金华起到了很大的影响。更多的人改变传统观念，以本土的传统技艺为基础，勇敢地走出这片世代居住的红土地，闯出一条靠"做手艺"和"做生意"谋生的道路。金华人最大的特征就是利益最大化，通过各种手工艺加工，将成本低的材料卖出高的价格。一张纸加工成剪纸艺术，竹子编织成竹工艺等。

Jinhua people began to seek new ways to survive. Many people pursued official position while farming and studying, and some large families funded family children to study using clan property. But few of them could become officials. Since the Southern Song Dynasty, Wu Learning (Jinhua school of thoughts) was popular. The scholar Lv Zuqian advocated realism, attaching great importance to industry and commerce, "Commerce is built on agriculture, and agriculture depends on commerce, we should complement each other but not harm each other." Chen Liang also proposed the combination of interests and simultaneous development of agriculture and commerce, which had a great influence in Jinhua. A growing number of people changed traditional ideas. On the basis of local traditional skills, they bravely walked out of the red land where they lived for generations, and found a road of "making crafts" and "doing business" to make a living. The biggest feature of the Jinhua people is the maximization of benefits. They can sell low-cost materials in high prices through the processing of various handicrafts. A piece of paper is processed into paper-cut work, and bamboo is woven into bamboo craft and so on.

　　在永康民间广泛流行着"打铜打铁走四方，府府县县不离康"的民谣，正是永康百工文化的真实写照。以前永康铁匠走街串巷，上门服务。一般都是师徒俩每人都挑着一副行头，师傅挑的是一些比较轻的工具，而徒弟挑的是一头有风箱的工具箱，另一头是装棉被和生活用品，这副担子足有八十到上百斤重。到一村后找一户人家落脚，摆开家伙，全村人存了好久的坏掉的破碗破缸都拿去给师傅修。家境好一点儿的，会直接请师傅住家里，提供饭菜，这叫作供师傅。

In Yongkang, the folk song "walk around the country while making copper and iron, every county and household could not be separated from Yongkang" is popular, which is a true portrayal of handicraft culture of Yongkang. In the past, Yongkang blacksmith walked around to provide on-site service. Generally, both the master and the apprentice carried their outfit, and the master carried some relatively light tools, while what the apprentice picked was a toolbox with bellows on one side, and quilts and daily necessities loaded on the other side. This load is eighty to one hundred kilograms heavy. When they reached a village, they found a family to settle, and laid out tools. The whole villagers took broken bowls and jars to the master which had been kept for a long time. The better-off family would directly ask the master to live at home and provide food. This is called "offering accommodation and food for the master".

先用风箱烧起炉子，再将一点儿杂铜、草灰等放在坩埚里，放进炉中熔化然后开始修补。除补锅、补铜壶外，凭永康手艺人的聪明才智和一双巧手，电筒、锁等都能随机应变加以修理。

First they lit the stove with bellows, put a little scrap copper, grass ash and so on in the crucible, and put it into the furnace for melting, then began to repair. In addition to repairing pot and copper kettle, with their ingenuity and a pair of skilled hands, Yongkang craftsmen can also repair torch and locks and so on.

如今，永康人做大做强了五金业，不再需要肩挑担子走街串巷。不仅外地客商来永康购买五金制品，五金城还将市场布点到其他县市，真正树立了永康人自己的行业品牌。

Today, the people of Yongkang make hardware industry bigger and stronger, and no longer need to carry outfit to walk around. Not only do foreign merchants come to Yongkang to buy hardware products, but also hardware city sets markets in other counties and cities, and therefore the Yongkang people's own industry brand is truly established.

东阳的手工艺群体叫作东阳帮,是以水泥匠、木匠、雕花匠、塑佛匠为主体的木雕建筑工匠群体。他们的手艺祖辈相传。竹匠一般又称为篾匠。篾匠师傅把竹丝横纵交织,形成一个个工艺品和生活用品。

The handicraft group in Dongyang is called Dongyang Business Group. It is the woodcarving craftsmen group with cement maker, carpenter, carving maker and Buddha-carving craftsman as the main part. Their workmanship was handed down from their forefathers. Bamboo craftsman cross woven bamboo strips to form all kinds of handicrafts and daily necessities.

东阳百工中,最引人注目的是木雕。明代时期,东阳木雕应用于建筑和家具装饰,迅速形成了较完整独特的手法和艺术风格。到清中期的嘉庆、道光年间达到鼎盛。故宫选用的东阳木雕艺人达百余人之多。木雕师傅还远涉香港、新加坡、泰国等东南亚地区。

The most striking of all sorts of crafts in Dongyang is woodcarving. During Ming Dynasty, Dongyang woodcarving was used in the decoration of architecture and furniture, quickly forming more complete and unique techniques and artistic style and reaching its peak in Jiaqing and Daoguang period in the middle of Qing Dynasty. More than 100 Dongyang woodcarving artists were chosen by the Forbidden City. Woodcarving handicraftsmen once went to the Southeast Asian regions such as Hong Kong, Singapore and Thailand.

金华古村落里面很多牛腿雀替都出自东阳木工之手。"牛腿"最初之时仅仅是一根支撑斜木的木杆。至明初期,木杆上出现稍做雕刻的竹节、花鸟、松树之类浅雕。到清代,"牛腿"逐渐演变成整块斜木雕刻,工艺日趋烦琐,讲究精雕细刻。到民国时,因受西方雕塑艺术的影响下,不乏刻画细微的经典写实之作。

A lot of brackets and sparrow braces in Jinhua ancient villages were made by Dongyang carpenters. "Bracket" was originally only a wooden pole supporting the oblique wood. In the early Ming Dynasty, the shallow carving such as bamboo, flowers, birds and pines appeared on a wooden pole. In the Qing Dynasty, "bracket" gradually evolved into a block of wood carving, and carving craft was increasingly elaborate, exquisite and intricate. In the Republic Period, due to the impact of western sculpture art, there appeared some subtle classic works of realism.

随着近代文化兴起，传统以木雕作为装饰的营造方式逐渐消失。东阳工匠们与时代同行，由上门加工转向工厂生产，主要制作家具陈设品，如箱柜架、宫灯、屏风等。初时设厂于杭州、上海，及后增设到香港、新加坡和其他一些地方，产品销往海外。

With the rise of modern culture, the traditional way of using woodcarving as decoration gradually disappeared. Dongyang craftsmen keep pace with the times, change from on-site processing to factory production, and mainly produce furniture furnishings, such as cabinet frame, lanterns, screens and so on. They set up factories in Hangzhou and Shanghai at the beginning, later in Hong Kong, Singapore and other places. Products are sold overseas.

木雕工艺这一传统在现在一代人身上发扬光大，出现了很多东阳木雕大师。

The tradition of woodcarving has been carried forward by the present generation, and a great number of Dongyang woodcarving masters have appeared.

已建成并投入使用的中国木雕城，拥有商铺 4800 余间，是国内最大的木制工艺品和木雕（红木）家具集散地，而东阳中国木雕文化博览城，规划建成以木雕文化为核心，致力于木雕产品研发、展示与交流。

The Woodcarving City of China has been built and put into use. With more than 4800 shops, it is the distribution center of the largest wooden handicrafts and woodcarving (mahogany) furniture in China. The

第五章　婺商　Chapter Five Wu Commerce

Woodcarving Culture Expo City of China in Dongyang is to be built, which will take woodcarving culture as the core, and is committed to research, development, display and exchange of woodcarving products.

明代义乌引种糖蔗，一些青皮糖蔗制成的蔗糖被称为"义乌青"。到了清顺治年间，贾维承从闽越地区摹制了榨糖车，自此义乌地区才开始熬制红糖。红糖市场开始出现之后。义乌佛堂镇因水运便利而成为主要的红糖集散地，不少外地客商来此购货。

The sugar cane was introduced and planted in Yiwu in Ming Dynasty, and some sucroses made of green sugar canes were called "Yiwu Green". In the Shunzhi-governed years in the Qing Dynasty, Jia Weicheng made sugar-making machine in Minyue region, From then on the Yiwu area began to brew brown sugar. After brown sugar market began to appear, Fotang town of Yiwu became the main distribution center of brown sugar as a result of convenient water transport, and many businessmen from other regions came here to purchase goods.

东部地区的乡村农户则多制取"派皮糖"，走上"鸡毛换糖"的道路。他们肩挑糖担，手摇拨浪鼓，用自制的糖换取居民家中的鸡毛等废旧钢铁以获取微利。鸡毛换糖的人又被称为敲糖帮，组织内部进行了严格的分工，新人还会有人指导。

Most farmers of the eastern part made "Paipi sugar" , and embarked on the career of "chicken feather for sugar". They shouldered sugar loads, waved rattles, and exchanged homemade sugar for chicken feathers and other worn-out copper and iron of the residents to obtain low profits. The people doing "chicken feather for sugar" were also known as "Qiaotang Group" , and there was a strict division of labor in the organization. The newcomers would be guided.

鸡毛换糖的行头很简单。开始用木桶装糖，后来改用篾篓减轻重量。在篾篓上放置一个加盖的方盘，上面放"糖饼"，"糖饼"上覆盖纱布罩，另备一把"糖刀"，一支坚木锥。

The outfit of "chicken feather for sugar" is very simple. The barrel was used as sugar load at first, and later the bamboo basket was used to reduce weight. A covered square plate was placed on the bamboo basket. "Sugar cakes" were put on the plate, and were covered with gauze cover. In addition, a "sugar knife" and a wooden cone were prepared.

明朝抗倭名将戚继光招用义乌兵万人,平倭以后,返回故乡。由于他们长期脱离农事,善于游走各方,遂利用"义乌青"制成糖块,奔走他乡,以卖糖为生,成为最早尝试鸡毛换糖的人群。

Ten thousand Yiwu soldiers were recruited by Qi Jiguang, the famous anti-Japanese general in Ming Dynasty. After defeating the Japanese pirates, they returned home. Because they were out of farming for a long time, they were good at walking around. Then they used the "Yiwu Green" to make sugar and walked around the country to sell sugar for a living, becoming the group who first attempted to do "chicken feather for sugar".

20 世纪 70 年代以后,义乌货郎担转化为提篮叫卖的商贩,他们以竹篮、箩筐、旅行袋、塑料布为工具,随地设摊,沿街叫卖。在某些地段聚集形成了最早的小商品市场。改革开放后,义乌不断建立专业市场。今天,义乌发展成为全国最大的小商品流通中心和著名的国际性商贸城市。

After 1970s, street vendors in Yiwu changed into vendors who hawked their wares in baskets in the streets, With their bamboo baskets, baskets, travel bags, plastic cloth as tools, they set up their stands and peddled in the street. They gathered in some areas to form the earliest commodity market. After the reform and opening up, Yiwu continues to establish professional markets. Today, Yiwu has developed into the largest commodity circulation center in China and the famous international commerce and trade city.

第二节 婺商 Wu Commerce

金华曾长期是农耕文明十分发达的地区,早在1万年前,这里有先民在这里种植水稻,但从两宋时期起,尤其是明清以来,商贸文化全面兴起,不断发展,成为婺文化的重要组成部分。从义乌等地货担贸易,到兰溪商帮的崛兴,再到今天名扬天下的义乌国际商贸城、永康中国科技五金城和东阳以横店国家级影视实验区为首的影视文化产业等,都折射出婺商文化与时俱进、不断创新的精神特征。

Jinhua used to be highly-developed in agriculture for a long time. Residents planted rice there ten thousand years ago. However, since Song Dynasties, after Ming and Qing Dynasties in particular, commerce and trade rose and developed into an essential part of Wu culture. From the vendor business in Yiwu to the rise of the business group in Lanxi, the world-renowned Yiwu International Commodities City, Yongkang • China Hardware City and the national Dongyang Film Industry, all these reflect that the Wu Commerce culture keeps up with the time and is constantly innovative.

一、婺商的历史发展 The Historical Development of Wu Commerce

古代婺商的崛起,可以说发端于唐、宋。至明万历年间,八婺大地的工商业已形成相当规模,交易兴旺。金华古代的工商业大抵起源于农副产品加工、手工业和陶瓷、纺织、造纸、印刷等传统产业。从唐、宋开始到明、清和民国时期,水路在八婺商人开拓市场当中起到极为关键的作用。

The rise of Wu Commerce originated from Tang and Song Dynasties. Till the Wanli period of the Ming Dynasty, the business in the eight counties of Jinhua had developed into considerable scale and the trade had boomed. The ancient commerce and trade dated back to the traditional industries like the agricultural and sideline products processing, handicraft industry, pottery, textile, paper-making, printing and etc. Starting from the Tang and

Song Dynasties and till the Ming and Qing Dynasties as well as the Republic Period, waterway had played a vital role in expanding markets among Wu merchants.

八婺大地因拥有兰江、衢江、婺江、义乌江、永康江、东阳江和武义江这些纵横交错的水路而迅速发展起来。据历史记载,鼎盛时期在兰江上扬帆而过的有数千艘客货两用的船只。兰溪因此成为南来北往各色货物的集散地,一度有"小上海"之称。

The eight counties of Jinhua boomed shortly due to the interconnected waterways, including Lanjiang River, Qujiang River, Wujiang River, Yiwu River, Yongkang River, Dongyang River and Wuyi River. According to historical records, thousands of passengers and freight ships sailed through the Lan River in its heyday. Thus, Lanxi with a name of "Small Shanghai" had become the distribution center for goods coming from every part of China.

兰溪与八婺大地其他各县的商业关系表现出一种相互依存的特点。兰溪当时市场上的商品价格是八婺大地的方向标。兰溪的繁荣可以说是由整个婺商群体创造的。据志书记载,在兰溪的婺商包括义乌商人、永康商人、兰溪商人和东阳商人等,同时还包括祖籍在宁波、绍兴、江西、龙游、福建和安徽等地的商人。在这些商人当中,人数最多的要数义乌商人,而资产最雄厚、影响最大的则是来自安徽的商人。

Lanxi interdepended with other counties of Jinhua in its business. The prices of goods in Lanxi market guided those in other counties. The prosperity of Lanxi could be said to be the collective success of Wu businessmen. According to historical records, the merchants in Lanxi include those from Yiwu, Yongkang, Lanxi and Dongyang, others from Ningbo, Shaoxing, Jiangxi, Longyou, Fujian and Anhui. Among these merchants, most of them came from Yiwu, while the most wealthy and influential businessmen were from Anhui.

不过,自从"民国"二十三年(公元 1934 年)高速公路和铁路开通后,内外货物改道分流,金华的经济枢纽地位日益显现,逐渐超过兰溪,成为浙中经济中心。"民国"二十五年(公元1936),金华与兰溪的商店数量已经持平。"民国"二十六年后(公元1937),上海、宁波、广州、汉口和杭州等地沦陷,浙江省政府及一些工商企业迁往金华等地,金华更加热闹,货物远销云南、贵州、四川等地,一度成为浙东南繁华的都市。

However, since the opening of new railway and highway in the 23rd year of the Republic of China (1934), the traffic of goods was rerouted and Jinhua, as the new economic hub, was increasingly self-evident. It gradually overtook Lanxi to be the economic center of Mid-Zhejiang. In the 25th year of the Republic of China (1936), the number of stores in Jinhua was equal to that in Lanxi. After the 26th year of the Republic of China (1937), cities like Shanghai, Ningbo, Guangzhou, Hankou and Hangzhou fell into enemy's hands, Zhejiang Provincial government and some businesses moved to Jinhua, making it even more bustling. With goods sold to places like Yunnan, Guizhou, Sichuan and so on, Jinhua once became a prosperous city in southeast Zhejiang.

二、婺商的资本运作　Capital Operation of Wu Commerce

旧时的婺商,资本来源多种多样,大致分为以下几种。一、共同资本,合伙经营。这是一种类似股份合作制的形式,在旧时婺商当中较为普遍。二、委托资本。由资本所有者授予资本给商人经营。这种现象在旧时婺商当中也较为普遍,所有权和经营权分离,由职业经理人来管理整个商店的业务和人事等。从"民国"二十八年(公元1939年)开始,义乌商人陈孝三首次出现在职业经理人的岗位上,打破了完全由安徽商人充当职业经理人的格局。三、劳动资本。比如义乌人就往往是从底层干起,等到积累了一定劳动资本后才一步步走向经商之路。另外,还有同乡会和亲戚资助的援助资本等。

The capitals of Wu Commerce came from diversified sources, which can be classified into the following types. ①Common capital, partnership.

Similar to shareholding Co-operative system, it was quite popular among Wu businessmen at that time. ②Entrusted capital. The owner of capital entrusted businessmen to run the business, which was also popular among the Wu businessmen. The ownership and management were separated, and professional managers were hired to supervise business and employees. Since the 28th year of the Republic of China (1939), Chen Xiaosan, a businessman from Yiwu, took the manager's position for the first time, breaking the tradition kept by Anhui businessmen, which was, all the managerial positions were taken by Anhui businessmen. ③Labor capital. For instance, Yiwu people usually started from the bottom, after they had accumulated a certain amount of labor capital, they would get on the way to do business step by step. Moreover, there were other capitals supported by associations of fellow townsmen and relatives.

而且，旧时婺商的经营能够做到审时度势、灵活多变。民国初期，一些工厂为了打开销路，规定进货者可以先提货，到月底结付货款。许多婺商利用这种进货特点，以微利经营争取快销。

In addition, the Wu businessmen at that time could seize up the situation and with a flexible operation. In early period of the Republic of China, in order to expand market, some factories would deliver goods in advance, while the payment could be settled until the end of the month. Many Wu businessmen made full use of such convenience to get very narrow margins for quick sales.

旧时婺商与婺商之间、批发商和零售商之间还出现了"以票兑币""赊销经营"的方法。

At that time, "document for money" and "sale-on-credit" also emerged among businessmen, wholesalers and retailers.

在兰溪的商人们，除了与外埠的商人存在资金往来以外，在本埠商人之间也有资金往来。由于彼此认识，一个店行开具的票可以到另一个不相同的店行兑换成钱币，木行的票可以到纸行的店里兑钱，而且从不赖账,也不会延期支付。这种"以票兑币"的方法基于彼此之间建立的诚信关系,给资金更大范围的运作奠定了基础,算得上是当代银行业的雏形。

Among the businessmen of Lanxi, capital transactions existed not only between local businessmen and those from other places, but also among the locals. Because they knew each other, the documents issued by one store could be exchanged into money in another store. The document of wood shop could be exchanged in a paper shop, which would never be denied or deferred in payment. Such "document for money" was based on mutual trust, paving the way for capital operation for a larger scale, which could be regarded as the prototype of banking.

"赊销经营"则是在安徽商人当中先做起来的,随后传给在八婺大地经商的其他商人。据说,赊销生意的对象主要为一村一乡或一镇一城当中的常年客户。对每个客户,均采用立户头、记账折的方法。客户只要拿着账签,就可以到店里购买产品或提货,不需要当场支付货款。这种方法也基于彼此之间建立的诚信关系。可以说,旧时婺商创下的成功经营经验,并不比当代婺商逊色。

"Sale-on-credit" first appeared among Anhui businessmen, and then it was spread to other businessmen working in the eight counties of Jinhua. It's said that the major targets of crediting business were regular clients in a village or in a town. For each client, an account would be set up and each transaction was kept on the account. The client could buy or pick up the goods with the account, requiring no immediate payment on the spot. This was actually based on mutual trust that was established among them. In other words, the successful business achievements of ancient Wu businessmen were no inferior to modern businessmen.

三、婺商文化的特色　Features of Wu Commerce Culture

婺商文化以义乌拨浪鼓文化、永康五金文化、东阳木雕文化和兰溪丹药文化为代表,具有深厚的传统底蕴和鲜明的技艺性、创新性、开放性特色，并对八婺商业的形成和发展产生了重要的影响。

The culture of Wu Commerce is represented by the rattle-drum culture of Yiwu, hardware culture of Yongkang, wood-carving culture of Dongyang and magical pellets culture of Lanxi, which boasts with profound traditional background and distinctive features like craftsmanship, innovation and openness, which has been playing an essential role in the development of Wu business.

1. 技艺性 Craftsmanship

"艺商"是婺商文化的最大特色。这方面，最具代表性的是婺瓷、金华火腿、金华酒、婺罗、东阳木雕等。婺瓷从东汉时兴起，到宋以后逐渐衰落。金华火腿在宋代就已经闻名，明代成为贡品，不仅有着独特的腌制技艺和风味，而且还引发了相关饮食文化的兴起和众多文人墨客的歌咏诗赋。以白蓼曲酿造的金华酒拥有独特的造曲方法、优化的用曲技艺、复杂的酿造程序和出众的品质，其酿造技艺堪称我国古代早期米酒酿造技艺的典型代表和完整文化遗存。婺罗是宋元时期有名的丝织品，为金华地区所独产，一度产量巨大，运销各地。东阳木雕是一种以平面浮雕为主的雕刻技艺，位居全国四大木雕之首，已被列为国家首批重点保护的传统工艺美术品种和国家级非物质文化遗产名录推荐项目。

"Craftsmanship Business" is the most prominent feature of Wu Commerce culture, whose the most representative are Wu porcelain, Jinhua ham, Jinhua wine, Wu silk and Dongyang sculpture. Wu porcelain rose from East Han Dynasty and gradually declined after Song Dynasty. Jinhua ham was well-known since Song Dynasty and became tributes in Ming Dynasty with its unique pickling technique and flavor. Besides, it triggered the rise of related food culture and intrigued men of letters started to write poems and articles. Jiuhua wine, brewed from Bailiao yeast, is the archetype of ancient brewing techniques of rice wine and intact cultural heritage, with its superior yeast technique, complicated brewing procedures and excellent qualities. Wu silk, exclusive products from Jinhua, was famous textile fabrics in Song and Yuan Dynasties, which was sold in many places with huge production. Dongyang sculpture, a type of sculpture technique in relief, ranked the first among the four woodcarvings nationwide. It has been listed in the first batch of traditional arts and crafts under special protection of the nation and National Intangible Cultural Heritage

2. 创新性　Innovation

婺商是一个勇于创新的群体,其在传统工艺上的创新为人们所公认,其在制度的创新上更是闻名遐迩。1790 年,兰溪祝裕隆布店首次委托"外人"经营商铺,并成立董事会(祝氏八房各派出一名代表),推举董事长(主事人)、委托总经理(经手)经营。除年终由主事人听取经手的经营状况报告,决定经手的去留外,平时一切经营权、人事任免权、奖惩权等,均由经手行使,祝氏家族一概不加干涉。体现出所有权与经营权分离的"两权分离"制度,据考证比西方还要早 51 年。当代婺商继承了古代婺商善于学习、勇于创新的优秀传统。如倪捷在 2002 年提出"学习海尔 创新绿源",当时就自封为公司的首席学习官,向员工推荐阅读《第五项修炼》,并且开始试着建立企业的学习制度等。

Wu Commerce is an innovative group, not only in traditional techniques, which is acknowledged by all, but also in management systems, which is renowned far and wide. In 1790, Zhuyulong Clothing Store in Lanxi first hired an "outsider" to run business and formed a board of directors (each household from the eight Zhu families assigned one delegate), with the chairman selected and the manager appointed to operate the business. In the year end, the manager would report the store's performances to the chairman, while the later decided whether the former should stay or leave. Except this, everything was in the charge of the manager, including operation, employment, praises and punishment, Zhu family would not interfere. The system of separating ownership and management is said to be 51 years earlier than that in the west. Modern Wu Commerce inherited the tradition of learning and innovation. For instance, when Ni Jie called on "Learn from

Haier, innovate Lvyuan" in 2002, he appointed himself the chief learning officer. He recommended his employees to read *The Fifth Discipline* and started to set up the learning system in the enterprise.

3. 开放性 Openness

就古代婺商而言,主要是行商为主。无论是"义乌一面鼓""永康一只炉""东阳一把斧""兰溪一剂药",都有走南闯北、走街串巷、走村串户的特色,形成了婺商"走南闯北、四海为家"的特性。也正是婺商的行商特点,使他们能主动走向市场去参与竞争,勇于走南闯北去寻找商机,跨出国门去开拓国际市场。他们凭着自强不息、甘于吃苦的精神,硬是在一个资源禀赋先天不足的地方培育出全球最大的小商品市场,培育出了"中国五金之都",成就了"建筑之乡"。

As for the ancient Wu merchants, their sole purpose was to do business. No matter the rattle-drum of Yiwu, the stove of Yongkang, the axe of Dongyang, or the pellet of Lanxi, they had traveled all over the country, going through streets and alleys, thus forming a feeling of being at home wherever they go. It is this characteristic of travelling businessmen that enables them to compete on the market, brave enough to travel from south to north to look for opportunities. They've even explored international market with perseverance and willingness to endure any hardships, breeding the largest global small commodities center, the largest National Hardware City and the Town of Architecture, in such a place with little resources and endowments.

第六章 婺州名产

Chapter Six Jinhua Specialties

婺州（今金华市）是历代官府治所，建制久远，古属越国地，秦入会稽郡，自三国吴元宝鼎元年（266 年）置郡始名东阳以来，具有 1 800 年的历史和灿烂文化。婺州素有浙江第二粮仓、中国金华火腿之乡、茶花之乡、佛手之乡、兰花之乡的美誉。

Wuzhou (present Jinhua), where the feudal authorities were located has a long history in governmental organization system. It belonged to the Yue State and was merged into Kuaiji County. Since it was established as Dongyang County in the first year of the Yuanbao Period in the Wu State (266 A.D) during the Three Kingdoms, it had a 1 800 years' history and splendid culture. Wuzhou has enjoyed such fames as the Second Largest Barn in Zhejiang Province, the Land of Ham, the Land of Camellia, the Land of Fingered Citron and the Land of Orchid.

第一节 自然名产 Natural Products

金华得天独厚的地理位置和气候环境创造了丰富的自然名产，其中以佛手、山茶花和兰花最具有代表性。

Because of the unique geographic position and climate, Jinhua has rich natural resources such as fingered citron, camellia and orchid, which are the most representative ones.

佛手是金华独有的地方特产,雅称金佛手,其果形状奇特美观,上部分裂成手指状,颇似佛祖的"兰花指",是我国一种珍稀佳果。它具有多种保健功能,尤以健胃、止痛、化滞、疏肝、理气为突出,古时就列为皇家贡品。佛手是十分顺应当今全球性"生态饮食"潮流的天然保健品。

Fingered citron is exclusive in Jinhua, also called golden fingered citron. It is a rare and valuable fruit, which is split like Fingers. It has special and beautiful looking like Buddha's orchid fingers. In ancient times, fingered citron was listed as royal tribute for its various health-care functions, such as promoting digestion, relieving pain, removing stagnated food, soothing liver and regulating flow of energy. Fingered citron is a global eco-food and can be used as a natural health-care product.

山茶花以优美的姿态,艳丽的花色闻名。由于山茶花娇美色艳,树叶鲜绿而四季常青,因此,深受人们珍爱。金华的土壤和气候,非常适宜山茶花的生长。金华有全国最大的茶花生产基地,金华市民喜欢在家中阳台、庭院栽种山茶花观赏,美化环境。1986年10月起,金华市人大常委会正式确定山茶花为金华市市花。

Camellia is famous for its elegant looking and bright color. With delicate and attractive flowers and ever-green leaves in four seasons, the camellia is loved by locals. The soil and climate in Jinhua are especially suitable for camellia. Jinhua has the biggest base of camellia in China. Citizens here like planting camellia in their balconies and courtyards to enjoy and beautify their living environment. The NPC standing committees officially named camellia as city flower of Jinhua in October,1986.

兰花自古以来就被人们尊称为"国香",与梅、竹、菊并列为"四君子"。兰花性喜温暖、湿润和通风良好、阳光不直晒的环境,兰溪盛产兰花,名贵品种颇多,其种质资源在省内乃至全国占有一定的地位和名气。1988年,兰溪市人民政府确定兰花为兰溪市市花,使兰花成为兰溪市的象征。

Orchids, renowned as the "National Fragrance" since ancient times, are known as one of the Four Gentlemen (together with plum blossom, bamboo, chrysanthemum). Orchids prefer warm, wet, well-ventilated and shaded environment. Lanxi owns such an environment which is good for growing orchids, therefore producing abundant valuable orchids, enjoying a position and fame in Zhejiang Province and even in China. In 1988, the government of Lanxi named orchids as the city flower and orchids became the symbol of Lanxi City.

第二节　手工制品　Hand-made Products

金华悠久的历史、传统的文化、质朴的民风创造出一批值得世人称道的手工制品，其中，以金华火腿、金华酥饼、义乌红糖和金华府酒最具有代表性。

There exists famous hand-made specialties in Jinhua with a long history, traditional culture and simple folk custom. Jinhua ham, Jinhua crispy cake, Yiwu brown sugar and Jinhua wine are the most representative ones.

火腿　Hams

火腿是由猪腿腌制而成的，火腿质量的优劣取决于生猪品种的好坏。金华地区农家饲养的"两头乌"，其以皮薄骨细，腿心丰满，肉质细嫩等优点成为火腿制作的最佳选料。唐开元年间（713-742年）文人编撰的《本草拾遗》中，就有"火腿产金华者佳"的记载。金华火腿由此誉满全球。

Hams are made from pig's legs, and their quality depends on pigs. The double-black-end pig is well-known in Jinhua and is used as the best raw materials for making hams, for its thin skin and bone, plump and tender leg meat. During the Kaiyuan period of the Tang Dynasty (713-742A.D.), a famous medical book named *Ben Cao Shi Yi* recorded that the ham produced in Jinhua is the best one. From then on, Jinhua ham became world-famous.

据传,"火腿"之名出自宋高宗赵构的金口。宋朝时,义乌的猪肉腌制业已相当普遍,一些富贵人家把它当作亲朋好友间的馈赠珍品。宗泽是义乌抗金名将。有一次回乡探亲返京的时候,乡亲争相送猪腿以做礼物,因为路途遥远,所以撒盐腌制以便携带。宗泽将这种经过腌制的猪腿奉献于朝廷。宋高宗见这种猪腿的肉,鲜红似火,煮食之,其味鲜美无比,遂赞不绝口,于是赐名"火腿"。从此"火腿"之名迅速在神州大地传开。因为宗泽朝贡的火腿产于义乌,而义乌属金华府管辖,遂把火腿取名为"金华火腿"。

It was said that an emperor, zhaogou, Song Gao Zong, in the Song Dynasty gave the name "Huo Tui" to the ham. In the Song Dynasty, pork salting industry was very popular in Yiwu. Some rich people took the salted pork, especially salted pig leg "Huo Tui" as gifts to relatives and friends. A famous general against Jin named Zong Ze was greatly honored by people. Once he visited his hometown—Yiwu. When he left for capital, people gave salted pig legs to him as gifts. Because it was a long way from his hometown to capital, salted pig legs were easy to keep and take. When Zong Ze arrived at capital, he presented the gifts to the Emperor Song Gao Zong. And the emperor gave the name "Huo Tui" to them because they looked like fire and were very delicious. From then on, "Huo Tui" became well known in the whole country. Zongze's hometown belonged to Jinhua Prefecture, "Huo Tui" is also called Jinhua Huo Tui.

金华酥饼是一道金华名点,它酥香可口,历来是金华人走亲访友的乡土礼品。金华酥饼表里酥脆,内荤外素,水分少,耐存放,是一种风味独特的糕点。古时秀才赶考,今人出门旅行,皆乐以此为干粮,宴请宾客则可作席间点心。金华酥饼以面粉、雪菜、肥肉、素油、芝麻、饴糖为原料,经多道工序制作而成。种类繁多,除传统的梅干菜肉馅酥饼之外还有火腿酥饼、甜酥饼、辣酥饼等。

第六章 婺州名产 Chapter Six Jinhua Specialties

Jinhua crispy cake is a famous snack in Jinhua officially. It tastes delicious and is taken as a local present to relatives and friends. It is a special dim-sum because of the crispy taste inside and outside the cake with meat inside and flour outside. It can be preserved for a long time because it is waterless, people would take it as food during the journey in ancient times For example, Xiucai, who passed the imperial examination at the county level in the Ming and Qing dynasties, was on a trek to the examination and when people go traveling in modern times, they would take it as food. People take Jinhua crisp cake as a snack when they entertain guests. With flour, pickled cabbgge，fat meet, vegetable oil, sesame and sugar as raw materials, Jinhua crispy cake is made through a variety of processes. There are a variety of Jinhua crispy cakes including Huo Tui crisp cake, sweet crisp cake and spicy crispy cake and so on, in addition to the traditional crispy cake stuffed with Meigancai, a kind of preserved vegetable.

红糖是义乌的拳头经济产品。数百年来，义乌红糖和义乌火腿和义乌南枣合称为"义乌三宝"。义乌生产的红糖甜味醇正，香气扑鼻，营养丰富，集糖品优点于一身，是红糖中的上乘佳品，行销全国各地，驰名省内外。义乌生产红糖的历史可以追溯到元末，至今已有 600 多年的历史。20 世纪 70 年代，义乌红糖曾经作为浙江省经济特产晋京进入中南海，受到党和国家领导人的赞赏。

Brown sugar is a representative economic product in Yiwu. It is one of the three most honorable products of Yiwu, the other two are Yiwu ham and Yiwu nanzao. It has good taste, sweet smell and rich nutrition. Yiwu brown sugar is superior and is welcomed around the whole country with great fame in Zhejiang and China. The history of Yiwu brown sugar could be traced back to the late Yuan Dynasty with a history of more than 600 years. In 1970s, as a local specialty of Zhejiang Province, Yiwu brown sugar was presented to the central government and was praised by leaders of the party and the country at that time.

金华酒历史源远流长,其酿造历史其实可以追溯到商周时期,春秋时期金华地区已经出现以糯米白蓼曲酿造的"白醪酒",首创了泼清、沉滤等工艺,提高了酒汁浓度,延长了贮存期。金华酒也叫寿生酒,今天业内和史学界专家们普遍认为,寿生酒工艺是我国古法白曲酿酒和当时新兴的红曲酿酒过渡型工艺的遗存,在世界酿造史上具有里程碑式的深远意义。

Jinhua Wine has a long histody which could be traced back to the Shang and Zhou Dynasties. In the Spring and Autumn Period, white wine mash made from sticky rice came into being in Jinhua district, with originating crafts like clearing and filtering, improving the quality and prolonging the storage time. Jinhua Wine is also called Shousheng Wine. Experts in both wine-making industry and historian circle believe that the making technology of Shousheng wine reflects the transition from the ancient white wine mash to the red wine making in our country and has had a far-reaching significance in the world wine-making industry.

唐代官府都设酝酿局,官府酒坊之酒专供公务饮用。"金华府酒"之名,即始于此。金华府酒品质出众,名驰遐迩,是唐时的名品官酒。

Authorities in the Tang Dynasty all set up a wine-making department to produce wine for official use. The name of "Jinhua wine" originated then. It got fame for its high quality and became the official wine.

金华酒所获荣誉无数。1915年,在美国举行的万国商品博览会上,金华酒与金华火腿同时获得金奖。1963年,在全国首届评酒会上,金华酒被评为优质酒,在黄酒系列中与绍兴加饭、福建陈缸齐名,是中国三大黄酒之一。

Jinhua Wine has got numerous honors. In 1915 at the International Commodities Fair held in USA, Jinhua Wine and Jinhua Ham both won gold medals. In 1963, Jinhua Wine was rated as Excellent Wine in the first National Wine-rating Meeting, being ranked as one of the three yellow wines in China, together with Shaoxing Jiafan Wine and Fujian Chengang Wine.

第六章 婺州名产 Chapter Six Jinhua Specialties

婺州菜特色鲜明，原料品质优良。菜品讲究原汁原味、香浓醇厚，饮食追求滋补，咸鲜、香鲜、咸甜、轻酸少甜微辣是婺州菜的主要味型。婺州菜既有古朴风格，又具时尚口感，适应性广，具有浓郁的地方风味，其中以火腿最为著名，是我国著名的八大菜系之一浙菜的重要组成部分，备受世人称道。金华菜中比较有代表性的有金华煲和两头乌扎肉。

Wuzhou Cuisine with distinctive features and good-quality raw materials emphasizes authentic and fresh flavor as well as nutrition. Its main- tastes include salty fresh, fresh, salty-sweet, slight acid, slight sweet and slight spicy. Being traditional but also modern, with intense local flavor, it caters to diverse tastes. As substantial resource in Zhejiang Cuisine, one of Eight Cuisines in China, Jinhua Ham is widely favored. The most representative dishes are Jinhua Pot and double-black-end pork.

金华煲作为金华本土的特色菜肴，在江苏、浙江、山东、湖南、广东、北京、上海、深圳等省市都极负盛名。金华煲里名气最大的是胴骨煲，胴骨自然得用金华特产"两头乌"，香味浓郁，而豆制品同样必不可少：千张香滑有劲，油泡香酥饱满。最好的胴骨是两头乌的后腿骨，猪后腿比猪前腿骨头粗，骨髓多，骨味自然更甘香。胴骨虽然几乎无肉，骨髓的味道却是极好的，插上吸管慢慢吮吸，将汤汁的浓郁和胴骨的鲜味一并入腹，这是胴骨煲最让人回味的地方。

Jinhua Pot, a local special dish, are well recognized in Jiangsu, Zhejiang, Shandong, Hunan, Guangdong, Beijing, Shanghai and Shenzhen. Tonggu (tube-bone pot) with the biggest fame uses the tube bone of double-black-end pigs and dried bean curd as raw materials. Dried pieces of bean-curd are aromatic, smooth and chewable. Puff paste are sweet, crisp and flush. The best tube bone is from rear leg of double-black-end pigs. The bone of a pig's rear leg is bigger than its fore leg, so there is more bone marrow in it, which intensifies the flavor. Although there is little meat in tube bone, the taste of bone marrow is incredible. You can put in straw sucker to suck the marrow and taste the aromatic soup and the fresh tube bone will rush to your stomach together. This wonderful feeling is most evocative.

　　"两头乌"是金华的特产,这种中间白、两头黑的猪皮薄骨细,肉质绝佳,两头乌扎肉的食材就是著名的两头乌。两头乌扎肉要与金华的寿生酒一起烹饪才能烧出这种肉香味糯,油而不腻的感觉。"入口即化"这词就是专门为这肉准备的,薄皮嫩肉,色泽红亮不说,酥烂入口却不觉油腻。金华圆馒头被认为是两头乌扎肉的绝配,把松软的馒头掰开放入肉,就能感觉到肉与油在舌尖的肆意游走了。

　　Double-black-end pigs are specialties in Jinhua. These pigs are black at heads and tails, and white in the body with very thin skin and slim bones. A famous dish named meat of double-black-end pigs is to cook with Jinhua wine to let it taste sweet, tender, rich but not greasy. It is so smooth that it would melt once in the mouth. It does not taste greasy at all. The dish with thin skin, tender meat and bright color, is suggested to eat with Jinhua round bun. You can tear the bun and put the meat in the middle of it, then you can feel the meat and fat melting at the tip of your tongue.

第七章　金华景观

Chapter Seven Jinhua Landscapes

第一节　人文景观　Cultural Landscapes

太平天国侍王府[①]　Site of King Shi's Residence of the Taiping Heavenly Kingdom

太平天国侍王府,原为唐宋时的州衙、清朝时的试士院,位于金华城东鼓楼里。1861 年太平天国侍王李世贤攻占金华后改建。太平天国侍王府是当年侍王的指挥中心,现为国家级重点文物保护单位。侍王府是太平天国的艺术宝库,存有众多艺术品,庭院中有五代时期钱镠时所植的古柏两株,至今枝繁叶茂,苍劲多姿,也是全国现存的太平天国建筑中保存最完整,规模最宏大,壁画等艺术品最多的一处。

The King Shi's Residence of the Taiping Heavenly Kingdom, the original state office of the Tang and Song Dynasties and the official choosing court, is located in the East Drum Tower, Jinhua. It was rebuilt after the King Shiwang of the Taiping Heavenly Kingdom, Li Shixian occupied Jinhua in 1861. The site of King Shi's Residence of the Taiping Heavenly Kingdom, which is the command center of King Shi is now a national key cultural relics protection unit. The site of King Shi's Residence is the art treasure place of the Taiping Heavenly Kingdom, with many works of art. There are two old cypress trees in the courtyard planted in the Qianliu of Five Dynasties period, now in a flourishing and vigorous state. It is also a place preserving the most complete and ambitious murals and other works of art of the existing Taiping Heavenly Kingdom buildings.

八咏楼 Eight Chant Tower

八咏楼位于金华城区东南隅,坐北朝南,面临婺江,原名玄畅楼。据光绪《金华县志》记载,系南朝齐隆昌元年东阳郡太守、著名史学家和文学家沈约建造。竣工后沈约曾多次登楼赋诗,写下了不少脍炙人口的诗篇。从唐代起,遂以诗名改玄畅楼为八咏楼。

The Eight Chant Tower is located in the southeast Jinhua City, facing south and Wujiang River Wu, formerly known as Xuanchang Tower. According to *Jinhua County Records* of Guangxu version, it was built by Shen Yue, a famous historian, writer and chief in Dongyang Prefecture in the first year of Qi Longchang in the Southern Dynasty. After its completion, Shen Yue has ascended many times to write poems, many of which are quite popular. From the Tang Dynasty, its name was changed from Xuanchang Tower to Eight Chant Tower because of the name of eight chants.

八咏楼自创建以来的一千四百多年中,与历代文人名士结下了亲缘。南宋著名爱国女词人李清照避难金华时,登八咏楼写下了《题八咏楼》诗。还有明末兵部尚书朱大典,率兵与清军激战中,壮烈地牺牲在八咏楼,留下了可歌可泣的英雄史迹。周恩来同志1939年到金华视察期间,也曾在八咏楼下的八咏滩头召开过近千人的群众大会,慷慨激昂地宣传团结抗战的方针。

In the history of more than 1,400 years since its construction, scholars of ancient literati forged a kinship with Eight Chant Tower. When Li Qingzhao, a famous patriotic woman poet of the Southern Song Dynasty took refuge in Jinhua, she composed a poem titled *Eight Chant Tower*. And Zhu Dadian, Minister of the Board of War in the late Ming Dynasty, in the course of fighting against Qing Dynasty army, sacrificed himself in the Eight Chant Tower, leaving a heroic history. When Zhou Enlai inspected Jinhua in 1939, he held a mass conference of over 1000 people at the beachhead of the Eight Chant Tower to disseminate the unity strategy in the anti-Japanese war.

郑义门古建筑群　Zhengyimen Ancient Buildings

在中国历史上，有一个家族历时长达三百五十多年，历经宋、元、明三代，被朱元璋赐名为"江南第一家"，这就是金华浦江郑氏，又称"郑义门"。在郑义门古建筑群中最有代表性的是郑氏宗祠。

In the Chinese history, there is a family lasting three hundred and fifty years in the Song, Yuan and Ming dynasties, named "The First Family in Jiangnan" by the emperor Zhu Yuanzhang. That is Zheng's family in Pujiang, Jinhua, also known as "Zhengyimen". The most representative one in Zhengyimen ancient buildings is Zheng's Ancestral Hall.

郑氏宗祠始建成于南宋，迄今已有 600 年历时。全祠门向西，面向白麟溪。入门后，右侧有一石碑，上书"白麟溪"，是元丞相所书，左边是一排苍劲古柏；旁边的水池称"洁牲池"，里面有两中小池，形成一个"品"字。一行古柏，一个品字，寓意"一品当朝"。整个郑氏宗祠可分为五进。前为师俭厅，次为中庭，三为有序堂，四为孝有堂，五为寝室，正位供奉同居列祖神位。

Zheng's ancestral hall was built in the Southern Song Dynasty, with a history of 600 years so far. The whole hall faces west and Creek Bailin. There is a stone on the right side named "Creek Bailin" by the Yuan prime minister after entering the gate, and a row of vigorous cypresses on the left. A pool named "Clean Pool" , locates beside with the formation of a "Pin" word. A line of cypresses, and a word of "Pin" means "first rank in the imperial court". The Hall can be divided into five parts. The first is for frugal hall, the second for atrium, the third for orderly hall, the fourth for filial hall, fifth for bedroom, and the orthodox dedicated to cohabiting ancestral tablets.

支撑"郑义门"的精神支柱，就是著名《郑氏规范》的家规。这是郑氏家族管家治家的法宝。它将儒家的"孝义"理念,如数学公式般转换成操作性极强的行为规范,涉及家政管理、子孙教育、冠婚丧祭、生活学习、为人处世等方方面面,堪称世上最齐全的家庭管理规范。

The spiritual pillar of supporting "Zhengyimen" is the famous *Zheng Norms*, which is Zheng family's core family administration. It transforms Confucian "Xiaoyi" concepts into strong operational norms like mathematical formulas, involving domestic management, education, marriage and funeral, life and study, how to conduct oneself and other aspects, regarded as the world's most complete family management practice.

智者寺 Zhizhe Temple

中国浙江省金华市智者寺又名智者广福禅寺、智者圣寿禅寺,俗称北山禅寺。位于金华山南麓,芙蓉峰(尖峰山)之西。始建于南梁普通七年(公元526年),是南朝梁武帝为"智者国师"——慧约法师所敕建的道场。是金华山历史上儒、释、道文化和谐共处的代表,是双龙国家级名胜区内著名的历史文化遗存。

The Zhizhe Temple is also called Ample Blessing Zhizhe Buddhist Temple, Sacred Longevity Zhizhe Buddhist Temple and North-Hill Temple. It locates in the south of Jinhua Mountain, in the west of Hibiscus Peak. It was built in the 7th year of Putong in Nanliang Period (526A.D.). It was built for the national wise man—Huiyu Cleric as a bodhimanda by the Liang Dynasty emperor. It's the representative of harmonious coexistence of Confucianism, Buddhism and Taoism in Jinhua's history and also the famous historical cultural heritage in the Double-dragon Cave National District.

智者寺在唐代建有大型的祝圣放生池,后又建有草堂、双清堂及雷音亭、倚松亭。唐代著名画家吴道子在智者寺的玻璃阁内画有《童真观音像》《释迦牟尼像》及《世支像》等,后均刻石勒碑。

In the Tang Dynasty, the Zhizhe Temple had a large Free Life Pond, and later-built Grass Tang, Shuang Qing Tang, Leiyin Pavilion, Lean-on Pavilion were constructed. Wu Tao-zi, the illustrious painter in the Tang Dynasty, painted *The Innocence Guanyin, The Sakyamuni Buddha, Shizhi* and so on, which were carved and tableted.

宋太宗赵光义于淳化年间 (990–994) 及至道年间 (995–997) 曾为智者寺两降御书共 120 卷。宋宁宗嘉泰三年 (1203 年)，方丈仲玘主持重修智者寺，著名诗人陆游为其撰写《重修智者广福禅寺记》，并以手迹勒石立碑，碑阴还刻有《与僧仲玘八札》。该石碑现保存于金华市太平天国侍王府内，为国家一级文物。

The Emperor Song Taizong bestowed works twice to Zhizhe Temple up to 120 volumes during Chunhua years (990–994) and Daoguang years (995–997). In Jiatai, the third year of Song Ningzong （1203）, the abbot Zhong Qi took charge of rebuilding the Zhizhe Temple. The well-known poet Luyou wrote *Rebuilding of the Ample Blessing Zhizhe Temple* for it which was carved and tableted later. The back of the stone tablet was carved with *Eight Letters to the Monk Zhongqi*. Now, the stone tablet was reserved in Site of King Shiwang's Residence of the Taiping Heavenly Kingdom in Jinhua city, regarded as the first-class national relics.

1958 年到 1985 年，因组建金华水泥厂（今尖峰集团），智者寺建筑群被陆续拆除，寺内文物也陆续遭到破坏和散失，目前仅尚存一块陆游撰写的千年古碑和一口千年古井。明代著名旅行家、文学家、地理学家徐霞客于 1636 年考察了金华山的智者寺、鹿田寺、双龙洞等，并详细记载于《徐霞客游记》。

From 1958 to 1985, the building group of Zhizhe Temple was torn down gradually and the cultural relic was destroyed and got lost because of Jinhua Cement Plant (Zhejiang Jianfeng Group), only remaining the stone tablet wrote by poet Luyou and a well with a history of one thousand years. Xu Xiake, famous traveller, writer and geographer, explored Zhizhe Temple, the Lutian Temple and the Double-Dragon Cave in Jinhua Mountain in 1636 and wrote it in *Xu Xiake's Travel Notes* with extremely specific information.

2008 年 6 月，浙江省民宗委批准复建智者寺；2010 年 5 月，智者寺复建工程正式奠基；2017 年 5 月，智者寺复建工程基本完工。

In June, 2008, Zhejiang Provincial People's Committee approved to rebuild Zhizhe Temple. In May, 2010, the rebuilding of Zhizhe Temple was laid a foundation. In May, 2017, the reconstruction was almost completed.

万佛塔　Wanfo Pagoda

万佛塔始建于北宋年间，是六角形楼阁式砖木结构密檐塔，因为塔身外壁每块砖上都雕有如来佛像，数以万计，故俗称"万佛塔"。每一块塔砖都是由当时的百姓供奉的。万佛塔一直作为金华的地标性建筑，直到抗战时期，国民政府为避免日军轰炸，迫不得已将万佛塔拆毁，1957 年在万佛塔下发现了地宫，出土了 183 个文物号的精美的文物，鎏金观音铜坐像最为精美，现存于中国国家博物馆内。

The Wanfo Pagoda constructed in the Northern Song Dynasty was a hexagonal pavilion with thick eaves and a half-timbered structure. On the external wall, each brick was engraved with an image of Buddha. It was called "Wanfo Pagoda" as there were tens of thousands of images of Buddha on the bricks of the Pagoda. Each brick was consecrated by the civilians. Wanfo Pagoda had been the landmark in Jinhua till the Anti-Japanese War. In order not to be attacked by the Japanese, the national government had to destroy Wanfo Pagoda. In 1957, an underground palace was found under the Wanfo Pagoda, where 183 fantastic cultural relics were unearthed. The gilded-bronze Guanyin Statue was the most exquisite and now it is preserved in the National Museum of China.

金华万佛塔地宫是南方出土地宫中最大，出土金铜造像最多，浙江出土佛像年代最早。现在发现地宫中唯一一个放有经幢的，也是唯一一个六面刻满经文的地宫。塔的地宫一般不大，多为 0.4 米左右，而金华万佛塔的地宫边长竟达到 1.57 米，六块石板筑成一个正方形地宫，六块石板刻满经文。

For the underground palace, it is the largest one unearthed in the southern China and has the most pieces of golden and bronze portraits unearthed. It unearthed the earliest figure of Buddha in Zhejiang. It is the only underground palace whose six walls are covered with stone pillar and the only building with lection all around. Normally, the underground palace under the Pagoda is not large, most which was about 0.4 m. But the underground palace of Wanfo Pagoda has a side-length of 1.57 meters. The six stones is used to build the square underground palace, fully carved with lections.

万佛塔始建于北宋嘉祐七年（公元 1062 年）的宝塔，素有"浙江第一塔"的美誉，明代的金华府治图和清代的金华府城图中都可以看到它醒目的身影，古时外地人来金华，无论是水路还是陆路，都能在城外很远的地方看到它的身影。而对于金华本地人来说，看到万佛塔就是看到了家。也正因为如此，万佛塔成了历代金华离乡百姓心中抹不去的乡愁，是金华城市的灵魂所在。

The wanfo Pagoda, built in 1062 A.D. (the 7th year of King Jiayou in the Northern Song Dynasty), is honored as the Top Pagoda in Zhejiang. It is vividly depicted in Jinhua Administrative Map drawn in Ming Dynasty and Qing Dynasties. In the past, those who came to Jinhua by waterways or land-ways could saw it far away, while locals took it as their home. And that is why the pagoda as the soul of Jinhua has been the irremovable place in their hearts.

黄大仙祖宫[②] Hometown of the Immortal Huang

黄大仙祖宫坐落于双龙鹿田景区内，风景秀丽的鹿湖东侧，坐北朝南，倚山望湖，湖畔常有云山雾海，蔚为壮观，呈现道教特有的神秘气氛。整个祖宫呈七进阶布局，从南向北依次为石照壁、石牌楼、灵官殿、钟楼、祭坛、鼓楼、大殿、三清殿、祈仙殿等。照壁对面的石牌楼全部用石板砌成，结构精巧，错落有致。祭坛是祖宫内宗教法事活动的主要场所。有趣的是，人站到坛中央鱼形太极图的中心喊一声，就能听到四面传来较大的回音，犹如站在谷底般。祭坛东西两面的钟楼和鼓楼，为四重檐结构，层层叠叠,富有道教特色。殿内的黄大仙神像座坛高 1.668 米,像高 5 米,整个神像由香樟精心雕刻彩绘而成,散发出阵阵清香。

The Hometown of Immortal Huang is located in the scenic area of Double Dragon Lu Tian, on the east side of the scenic Lake Deer, facing south, leaning against mountains and looking over lakes. There is often a spectacular sea of brume, exhibiting Taoism's unique mysterious atmosphere. The ancestral palace is in a seven advanced layout, from south to north in order of Stone Wall, Stone Arches, Lingguan Palace, Bell Tower, Altar, Drum Tower, Hall, Three-Qing Palace, Pray Fairy Palace, and etc. Stone walls opposite the stone archway are all built by slates, in compact and well-proportioned structure. Altar is the main place of religious activities in the ancestral palace. Interestingly, if one stands in the central fish-shaped Taiji map of the altar shouts, loud echoes will be heard from all sides, as if standing at the bottom of the valley. Bell Tower and Drum Tower on the east and west side of Altar respectively are in four-eave structure, layer upon layer and full of Taoism. The statue altar of Immortal Huang in the hall of the statue is 1.668 meters in height, and statue is 5-meter high. The entire statue is carved and painted carefully by the camphor, emitting bursts of fragrance.

黄初平(约 328- 约 386),后世称为"黄大仙",是中国民间信仰之一,著名道教神仙。出生于浙江省金华兰溪黄湓村。黄大仙原是当地的一名放羊的牧童,在金华山中修炼得道升仙。黄大仙传说在港澳台、东南亚等地流传甚广。今得道升仙地建有浙江金华黄大仙祖宫、广州和香港等地建有黄大仙祠。

Huang Chuping (328 A.D.–386 A.D.) is holy admired as "Huangdaxian", one of Chinese folk beliefs and also the famous Taoist Immortal. He was born in Lanxi Huangpen village of Jinhua, Zhejiang. He was a local shepherd boy, and later practiced austerities and finally attained the Way and became an immortal. The legend of Huangdaxian widely spreads over Hongkong, Macao, Taiwan and Southeast Asia. There established Hometown of Immortal Huang at the place where he attained the Way and became an Immortal, and there are memorial temples in Guangzhou and Hongkong.

叱石成羊　Transforming Stones into goats

传说黄大仙14岁那年去放羊,遇到一位道士,道士把他领到金华山的石屋里修炼,一晃就是40年。他的哥哥黄初起找到他,问他羊到哪里去了,黄初平说在东山,兄长一看全是石头,黄初平叱石成羊,顿时就有几万只羊。这只是其中一个流传了一千多年的民间神话传说,是来自金华北山的成语,也是黄大仙信仰的经典。明末传播到广东地区,清末传到港澳地区。黄大仙信仰传入中国台湾和东南亚及世界各地。成为侨胞同系的中华名族之根,也是国家级非物质文化遗产。

There is a legend that when Huangdaxian was herding goats, he encountered a Taoist who guided him to practice being immortals. After 40 years, his brother found him and asked him where sheep were. He replied that sheep were on Dongshan mountain. However, his brother found no goats but stones. Huang Chupin then transformed stones into goats, and tens of thousands of goats came out. This is only one folk legend passed down about 1,000 years, a legend of phrase of Beishan Jinhua, and also the classic belief of Huangdaxian. The belief in Huangdaxian was then widely popularized. It was introduced to Guangdong in the late Ming Dynasty, Hong kong and Macao in the late Qing Dynasty, and then to Taiwan, Southeast Asia and even all over the world, becoming the root of the Chinese nation. Today, Legend of Huangdaxian is listed among National Intangible Cultural Relics.

丽泽书院③　Lize Academy

丽泽书院是南宋著名哲学家、史学家、文学家、教育家吕祖谦讲学会友的场所,原址是其曾祖父吕好问携全家自开封迁居金华时借居的官屋。后来吕祖谦将官屋归还,另置新居于城北,丽泽堂随之北移。从南宋始建丽泽书堂,至明末毁于兵火,丽泽书院共存478年。吕祖谦治学严谨、著述颇丰,后其著作被清朝纪晓岚征集,编进了《四库全书》。丽泽书院名扬全国,生徒众多后有"明招学者""丽泽诸儒"之分,丽泽之学传之后世。

Lize Academy was the site for Lv Zuqian, a famous philosopher, historian, litterateur and educator in the Southern Song Dynasty, gave lectures and meeting friends. The site was originally an official house borrowed by his great grandfather Lu Haowen bringing the family from Kaifeng to Jinhua. Later, Lv Zuqian returned the official house, and bought another one in the northern city, and Lize Academy moved to the north after that. From the building of Lize Academy in the Southern Song Dynasty to its ruin by the war fire at the end of Ming Dynasty, Lize Academy lasted 478 years. Lv Zuqian has a rigorous scholarship, and quite abundant works, which was compiled into the *Si Ku Quan Shu* by Ji Xiaolan in the Qing Dynasty. Lize Academy was famous throughout the country and had a large number of students. With the separation of "Ming Scholars", "Lize Scholars", Lize scholarship was passed down from generation to generation.

仁山书院 Renshan Academy

仁山书院位于兰溪市芝堰乡,是清道光年间的建筑。书院坐北朝南,总体布局为前院、三进、两厢房,呈方形,建筑平面呈 T 形。一进,面阔三间,进深为七檩,明间梁架五架梁前后单步,为直梁,角柱为讹角青石方柱。天井两侧为过廊。二进,面阔、梁架、梁形及角柱均与一进样同。三进,面阔五间,进深为五檩,两侧各设三间厢房,自成小院落。

Renshan Academy is located in Zhiyan Town, Lanxi City, a building of the Qing Dynasty. The academy faces south, with the overall layout of the front yard, three parts, two rooms, in a square form and "T" shaped architectural plane. In the first part, there are three rooms, deep into seven purlins, and the beam frame between the five beams before and after the single step, straight beam, angle column for the angle bluestone side column. Corridors are on both side of the patio are. In the second part, widths, beams and angle columns are as the same as those in the first part. In the third part, there are five widths, with five purlins, and with three rooms on both sides, forming a small courtyard.

金华古城　Jinhua Ancient Town

金华古城是金华城市的发源地,距今已有 1700 多年历史。古子城是金华最具文化底蕴的地方,这里的每一幢老屋、每一口水井、每一块石碑都带有深深的历史烙印。古子城区域内有太平天国侍王府、八咏楼、天宁寺、徐家故里等大一批明清古民居 , 还包括一批国家、省、市级文物保护单位和历史文化遗存。

Jinhua Ancient Town is the birth place of Jinhua urban area, with a history of more than 1700 years. It is the place with most profound cultural contents. Every old building, every well and every stone here boasts a long history. It is home to a great many ancient residences of China's Ming and Qing Dynasties, such as King Shi's Residence of the Taiping Heavenly Kingdom, Bayong Tower, Tianning Temple, Xu's Residence, etc. It also contains a number of historical heritages and cultural relics protection units of state, provincial and municipal levels.

第二节　自然景观　Natural Landscapes

双龙洞景区　Double Dragon Cave Scenic Spot

双龙洞位于双龙景区洞前村附近,海拔约 520 米。双龙洞是风景区的代表性经典,由内外两个大洞及一个耳洞组成。洞口轩朗,两侧分悬的钟乳石一青一黄,酷似两龙,双龙洞头,两龙头在外洞,而龙身却藏在内洞,故名双龙洞。外洞洞厅高达 7～10 米,面积 1200 平方米左右,可容千人,气温常年保持在 15 摄氏度左右,是炎夏游人休息乘凉的最佳之处。外洞与内洞相距仅 5 米,有一巨大石屏相隔,仅留长 10 米,宽 3 米多的地下河道。水道水面离地下河顶灰岩仅有 0.30 米左右的间隙,进内洞需仰卧小舟而入。

The Double-Dragon Cave is located in the scenic area near the Dongqian village, at an altitude of about 520 meters. Double-Dragon Cave, the typical representative of the scenic area, consists of the two caves inside and outside and an ear-like cave. The cave is broad, with the hanging of a green and a yellow stalactites on both sides, resemble two dragons. Two dragon heads are outside, and dragon bodies are hidden in the cave, so it is named "Double Dragon Cave". The hall of the outside cave is up to 7-10 meters, with an area of 1200 square meters. Accommodating thousands of people, and maintaining at around 15 degrees Celsius, it is the best place for people to rest and shade in hot summer. The outside cave is only 5 meters apart from the inside cave, separated by a huge stone screen, leaving only 10 meters long and 3 meters wide underground river. The waterway surface is only 0.30 meters from the top limestone of the underground river, and therefore, people should lie in a boat if they plan to go inside the cave.

冰壶洞因口小肚大形似酒壶又凉气袭人而得名,因拥有全国最大溶洞瀑布而闻名。洞体垂深 70 余米,洞中瀑布位于洞口向下 50 米处,从暗河飞泻而出,丰雨时流量达 200 升 / 秒以上,落差高近 20 米,其势壮观无比。

The Ice-pot cave is reputed forits teapot shape and cool environment, and for its largest cave waterfall in the country. The depth of cave is more than 70 meters, and the waterfall is located 50 meters down from the cave mouth, with underground river flying out. When the rain flow is 200 liters per second or more, the gap is nearly 20 meters high, and its spectacular is incomparable.

永康方岩　Yongkang Noseanite

永康方岩是我国境内发育最充分、特征最鲜明的丹霞地貌区之一。它以其丹霞奇境、人文奇观、庙会奇俗吸引着广大游客慕名而来。方岩高 400 米,方圆约 3 000 米。方岩附近的山,都是绝壁陡起,孤峰独峙。洞奇石怪,瀑美水秀,置身于丹霞峰林,确有飘然欲仙之惑。

Yongkang Noseanite is one of the most developed and characteristc Danxia landforms in China. It attracts a vast number of visitors with its

Danxia wonders, human wonders and fair exotic customs. Noseanite is 400 meters high, with a radius of about 3,000 meters. Mountains near noseanite have steep cliffs and isolated peaks standing out. Exposed to the Danxia peak forest with strange cave rocks, and glamorous waterfall, there is indeed an illusion of being immortality for tourists.

　　方岩寺庙有数十座多，几乎无一例外地建在大大小小的岩洞之中，形成了国内独一无二的岩洞寺庙群。方岩最奇特的人文现象首推胡公。在人民群众心目中，胡公是"有求无不应，有祷无不答"的大帝，是人民群众的保护神、幸福神。

There are dozens of noseanite temples built in large and small caves almost without exception, forming a unique cave temple group. The most peculiar humanistic phenomenon of noseanite is Hu Gong. In people's mind, Hu Gong is the great, protection God and happiness God who can answer and fulfill people's requests and wishes.

　　方岩庙会起源于祭祀胡公活动，至今已有一千多年历史。庙会期间，永康及周边县市的民众以村为单位组成"罗汉班"，按照排定的日程到方岩表演。有的打拳舞棍，演练十八般武艺；有的吹拉弹唱，载歌载舞。

The Noseanite fairs originated in the ritual public activities in memory of Hu Gong, has a history of one thousand years. During the fair, villagers of Yongkang and surrounding counties organized a "Luohan Team" to perform shows like boxing, dance and swing sticks, performing various martial arts, and others blow, sing and dance.

磐安花溪风景区　Pan'an Huaxi Scenic Area

　　磐安县地广人稀，森林茂密，大小山峰 5200 余座，大气质量和 99 % 的河道水质常年达到国家一类标准，是古代名士隐居的世外桃源。磐安的山大都边缘陡峭，而山顶开阔平缓似高台，山间溪流纵横，峡谷连绵，瀑潭成群，鱼虾众多，景区大都以溪为名。夏季，游客们都喜欢在浅浅的溪中行走，或卧溪中顺水漂流。

In Pan'an County, people are sparsely populated in vast lands, with dense forests, and more than 5200 mountains in different sizes. Air quality and 99 % of the river water reach a national Astandard, and it is a seclusion paradise for ancient celebrities. Mountains in Pan'an are steep, while tops open like a flat high platform. Streams roll among mountains, valleys are shoulder in shoulder, waterfall pools group together and fish and shrimps are varied. Most scenic areas are famous for creeks. In summer, tourists would like to walk in the shallow river, or lie in the river drift.

平板长溪呈二处出现，一处为石下村，长约 100 米左右。另一处在花溪村南侧，总长 3000 米，宽 10 至 15 米不等。河床为平坦光洁的岩石，溪内流水晶莹，清澈见底，丽阳照射，水光激滟。临溪而观溪底，金灿灿犹如花岗岩铺设。经专家考察后确认，此平坦河床为一亿年前中生代火山喷发产状近于水平的似层状流纹岩，具有很高的观赏及科学考察价值，为世所罕见的自然奇观。

There are two Flat Slate Long Creeks. One is in the stone village, about 100 meters long, and the other is on the south side of Huaxi village, with a total length of 3,000 meters, ranging from 10-15 meters wide. The river bed is covered with smooth and clean rocks, with crystal and clear streams flowing. The water surface glitters under the sunshine. Viewing the bottom by the creek, one can see the creek is like a golden granite. After investigation by experts, it was confirmed that this flat riverbed was a nearly stratigraphic rhyolite of the Mesozoic volcanic eruption about 100 million years ago. It has high ornamental values and scientific investigation values, and is a rare natural wonder.

仙华山 Mountain Xianhua

仙华山又名仙姑山，位于浦江县城北 9 千米处，总面积 18 平方千米。主峰少女峰，海拔 728 米，相传因轩辕黄帝小女儿元修在此修真得道升天而得名。

Mountain Xianhua, also known as Mountain Celestial, is 9 kilometers from the northern Pujiang County, has a total area of 18 square kilometers.

The main peak Maiden is at an altitude of 728 meters. It is named according to the legend that the smallest girl of Xuan Yuan, Yellow Emperor self-cultivated here to ascend to heaven.

　　仙华山以奇秀的山巅峰林为胜,在海拔 600 米以上的仙华山巅,石峰耸峭壁立,拔地而起。仙华峰林尤以少女峰、仙坛峰、玉尺峰、玉圭峰、玉笋峰五峰最为雄伟灵秀。少女峰极险削,有登道铁链可供攀登。顶有平台,睛光灿烂,仙华八景之一的"华柱丹光"即此。仙坛峰,俗称二岩,海拔 700 米,多奇花野草,传为少女为民治病采药炼丹处。玉尺峰,海拔 672 米,又称中峰,此峰有扶云挟月之势,游人罕登,仙华八景之一的"中峰啸月"即此。

Mountain Xianhua is known for its unique peak. At an altitude of 600 meters above Mountain Xianhua, stone peaks stand towering, rising from the ground. Peak Maiden, Peak Sendai, Peak Jade, Peak Jade Gui and Peak Yusun are the most magnificent sceneries in the Peak Xianhua. Peak Maiden is dangerous, with chains for climbing. On the top there is a platform with bright sunshine which is known as "Hua-chu Dan Light", one of the eight scenes in Xianhua. Peak Sendai, commonly known as the Two Rocks, is at an altitude of 700 meters, with many exotic flowers and weeds. It was said to be the maiden's place for gathering herbs and alchemy for people's medical treatment. Peak Jade, 672 meters above sea level, also known as the middle peak, has the trend of handling clouds and carrying on the moon. There are seldom visitors, known as "Howling in the Middle Peak Moon" of eight scenes in Xianhua.

第三节　现代建筑　Modern Architecture

中国婺剧院　China Wu Opera Theatre

中国婺剧院,位于浙江省金华市区金华江、义乌江、武义江三江交汇的燕尾洲公园,由浙江婺剧艺术研究院（浙江婺剧团）负责管理,是燕尾洲城市文化艺术中心的核心建筑，2013年建成使用,是集歌剧、舞剧、戏剧、交响乐、音乐会、综艺演出等功能于一体的综合性文化中心,金华市标志性建筑之一。

China Wu Opera Theatre lies on Yanweizhou Park, where Jinhua River, Yiwu River and Wuyi River converge. Under the administration of Zhejiang Wu Opera Art Research Institute, it is a core building for city cultural and art center of Yanwei zhou Park. Being put into use in 2013, the theatre has become a symbolic building in Jinhua, integrating the functions for staging opera, dance drama, play, symphony, concert and comprehensive performances.

金华博物馆　Jinhua Museum

金华市博物馆位于浙江省金华市区东市街与将军路交叉口,总建筑面积13600平方米,其中展厅面积4700平方米。设有5个展厅,分从地质学角度解读金华的"神奇大地"展厅、从古村落角度解读金华的"乡土民风"展厅、从工商文明角度解读金华的"百工之乡"展厅和从文学艺术角度解读金华的"诗书传家"展厅。金华市博物馆是一座集教育、收藏、研究功能于一体,弘扬和传承优秀传统文化、展示历史遗存、传播文博知识的地市级综合性博物馆,是金华市重要的历史文化地标,精神文明窗口。

Jinhua Museum, locating at the intersection between St. Dongshi and Jiangjun Road, has a total building area of 13600 square meters, including the exhibition area of 4700 square meters. There are 5 exhibition halls with unique style. The hall of Amazing Earth is the interpretation of geography, the hall of Local Customs is the interpretation of historical villages, the hall of Handworks is the interpretation of business and merchandises and the hall of Poem is the interpretation of arts. Jinhua Museum, a comprehensive museum providing functions of education, collection and research, showing historical legacies and publicizing cultural information, is the important historical and cultural landmark and a show-window of spiritual civilization.

金华彩虹桥 Jinhua Rainbow Bridge

金华城区,有一座彩虹桥,横跨婺江两岸。这座桥,其实叫板凳桥,奉献这一独特创意的是北大城市与区域规划教授、著名景观设计大师俞孔坚,他的这一设计灵感源于金华当地民俗文化中的板凳龙,形态上仿其盘旋扭转,色彩上选取红黄炽烈,彰显了金华人蓬勃、团结、热情的精神面貌。这彩色舞动的板凳桥,更像一座彩虹,横跨在婺江之上,将江南和江北链接了起来。站在这座桥上,可以看到城市霓裳灯火照射在江面上的倒影,波光粼粼的水面上,偶尔还会有几艘游船;从桥上回望,那婺州江边茂盛的各类绿化乔木,若隐若现的闪烁着市区各类的灯光,更体现出"不出城廓而有山水之怡,身居闹市而有林泉之致",成为金华最富有诗意的都市"留白"。

In Jinhua urban area, there is a rainbow bridge with another name "bench bridge", crossing the both sides of Wujiang. Its unique creation is made by Yu kongjian, a professor at Urban and Regional Planning Department of Peking University. The design is inspired by the bench dragon in local Jinhua folk culture. As for the shape, the design imitates the bench dragon whirling and spiralling. As for the color, it selects blazing red and yellow, delivering the vigorous, united and enthusiastic personalities of people in Jinhua. The colorful and dancing bench bridge is more like a rainbow, crossing over the Wujiang and connecting the south side and north side of it. Standing on the bridge, we can see the beautiful shadow of the city lights. On the flickering water surface, there are several pleasure boats sailing occasionally. Looked back from the bridge, all kinds of lush green trees by the river the various looming lights in the city, can be seen, through which that we can enjoy the pleasure of mountains, rivers, forests and springs within the city gallery, which has become the most poetic urban atmosphere of Jinhua.

横店影视城　Hengdian World Studios

横店影视城，是集影视旅游、度假、休闲、观光为一体的大型综合性旅游区，被评为国家 AAAAA 级景区。它也是中国唯一的"国家级影视产业实验区"，被美国《好莱坞》杂志称为"中国好莱坞"。

The Hengdian World Studios, awarded as a national AAAAA scenic spot, is a large-scale comprehensive tourist area that integrates movie and TV tourism, vacation, leisure and sightseeing. It is also the only "experimental area of national film and television industry" in China and is called as "China's Hollywood" by the American magazine *Hollywood*.

横店诞生大片最多的地方，莫过于秦王宫。景区占地面积 800 亩，建筑面积达 11 万平方米，造型恢宏大气，秦汉风格浓郁。有雄伟壮观的王宫宝殿 27 座，主宫"四海归一殿"高达 44.8 米，面积 17169 平方米。长 2 289 米，高 18 米的巍巍城墙与王宫大殿交相辉映，淋漓尽致地表现出秦始皇并吞六国，一统天下的磅礴气势。

The place that produces the most blockbusters in Hengdian is the Qin Dynasty Palace. The covering area and building area is 800 mu and 110,000 square meters respectively. Its shape filled with a Qin-and-Han style is grand. There are 27 majestic palaces. The main palace "Sihaiguiyi palace" is 44.8 meters high and with an area of 17169 square meters. The lofty city wall, with length of 2 289 meters and height of 18 meters, is merged with the palace, thoroughly showing the tremendous momentum that the First Emperor of Qin merged the six countries and unified the whole country.

清明上河图拍摄基地参照于我国北宋著名画家张择端所绘《清明上河图》长卷，于 1998 年 11 月建成。其占地约 53 公顷，建筑面积近 10 万平方米。建有房屋 120 幢，桥梁 6 座，码头 9 个，船只 6 艘，牌坊 14 座。景区分外城、里城和宫城。

The Riverside Scene at Qingming Festival studio refers to the "Riverside Scene at Qingming Festival" scroll drawn by the famous Northern

Song painter Zhang Zeduan, and was completed in November 1998. The covering area and the building area is about 53 hecares and 100,000 square meters respectively. There are 120 houses, 6 bridges, 9 wharves, 6 boats and 14 memorial gates. The scenic area is divided into outer city, inner city and palace city.

注释：

① Source: https://baike.baidu.com/item/%E5%A4%AA%E5%B9%B3%E5%A4%A9%E5%9B%BD%E4%BE%8D%E7%8E%8B%E5%BA%9C/3818625?fr=aladdin

② Source:http://www.baike.com/wiki/%25E5%258F%258C%25E9%25BE%2599%25E6%25B4%259E%25E5%259B%25BD%25E5%25AE%25B6%25E6%25A3%25AE%25E6%259E%2597%25E5%2585%25AC%25E5%259B%25AD.

③ Source: http://www.jhnews.com.cn/2016/0102/589033.shtml 中文有修改。

第八章 金华古村落

Chapter Eight Jinhua Ancient Villages

第一节 古村落简介 Profile of Ancient Villages

村落布局与乡村建筑 Layout and Architecture

金华丘陵广布,村落在临水背山的开阔地选址,沿河流自然伸展。族群以血缘为纽带聚居。他们重视人与自然和谐,世代相承,居住繁衍。现存村落格局相对完整,砖、石、木雕精美绝伦,成为珍贵的文化遗产。

Jinhua has widespread hills. Villages are set up alongside mountains and rivers, and extend along both sides of rivers. The ethnic groups with blood relationship live together. They emphasize the harmony between man and nature, and live through generations. Here preserves relatively complete village structure and beautiful bricks, stones and wood carvings. Now, these have become precious cultural heritage.

金华村落选址与建筑布局强调顺应自然、因地制宜。人们通过筑堰引流、挖塘构桥,建庙宇、造楼阁,在水道进出口处植树,改变入口朝向等方法来改善人居环境。

The site selection of Jinhua villages and the layout of construction emphasize on following the nature, adopting measures to suit local conditions. People improve the environment of the village to flee from evil, and strive to walk in fair fortune's way through the measures like building weir, drainage, building bridges, digging ponds, building temples and pavilions, planting trees on the exit and entrance of waterway and changing the orientation of the entrance, etc.

建筑与装饰　Construction and Decoration

金华古村落最显著的特点是独特的建筑结构与精美的艺术装饰。精湛大气的门楼、肃穆敞亮的厅堂、精雕细琢的构件，这些具有鲜明地方特色，包含丰富历史文化信息的建筑与装饰，多出自本地工匠之手。

The most striking feature of Jinhua ancient villages is the unique building structure and the delicate art decoration. These buildings and decorations with distinctive local characteristics and rich historical and cultural information--the beautiful and grand gates, solemn and bright halls and the precisely-carved components--are constructed by the local wood craftsmen.

宗族结构与管理体系　Clan Structure and Management System

为维持乡村秩序，每个宗族都有族规，这是族人必须恪守的行为准则，以"敬宗收族"为目的，维系着宗族成员间的和睦共处和团结稳定。管事会是族规的实际执行者，肩负组织和管理宗族事物的职责，其成员由族内推举产生，负有相应的职责。

In order to maintain daily order in the village, each patriarchal clan has regulations as standards of conducting that clansmen must abide by. The regulations maintain the peaceful coexistence of clansmen so as to respect the authority and management of the clan. The committee of clan stewards as the implementer of regulations and rules is responsible for organizing and managing the clan affairs. Members of the committee recommended by the clansmen shoulder corresponding responsibilities.

拥有血缘关系的人群，聚居在一起并遵守一定的制度和规则，被称为宗族。血缘是宗族成员的自然纽带，一般按父系血缘关系，宗族可划分出不同的支派、房分。我们知道,古代最小的行政建制是县。县以下的村是宗族自治的。一般族人推举产生管事,管事成立管事会,分管族内各项事务,而由此组成的宗祠管事会则是维护宗族日常运作的组织核心。大宗祠管事会由族内功名最高、辈分最长、年龄最大、最有权威的人组成。所以说,古代大的家族宗族自制系统是非常完善的。为了方便管理,每个宗族会设自己的族规家规。例如浦江郑义门,15世同居,历经宋、元、明三朝。最多聚居有三千三百多人。要管理起这么多人,必须要有一套完善的规章制度。当时明太祖向义居第八世郑濂问治家长久之道。一国之君向一家之长请教治理方法。郑濂当时拿出的就是《郑氏规范》。

The people with kinship who inhabit a region and follow the same set of rules and systems are called clan/family system. Kinship is natural bond for clan members. According to the patriarchal kinship, the clan can be divided into diverse branches. As we know, the smallest administrative system was county, and villages under county was governed by the clan. As the core of regular management, the administrative committee of stewards recommended by clansmen took charge of all affairs. The stewards in the committee were from clansmen of highest official rank, the highest authority and the eldest, and therefore, there was a perfect autonomous system in the past. Each family system had their rules for a better management. Taking Zhengyimen in Pujiang for example, 15 generations lived through three Dynasties of Song, Yuan and Ming, among which there were a maximum of over 3,300 clansmen living together. He who managed so many people must have had a perfect system of rules and regulations. It is said that Emperor Zhu Yuanzhang of the Ming Dynasty asked the 8th generation Zheng Lian for advice on running a family. Zheng Lian answered with a book called *Zheng's Family Norms*.

一般大的宗族里分工非常明确,它分为族长和家长。一族之长为族长,管理宗族的大小事务,一家之长为房长,管理一家的大小事务。明朝由于监生私纳赃款,篡改丈量田地的鱼鳞图册,导致当时担任一方粮长的浦江郑氏家族的族长郑濂因失察而获连坐之罪。刑部差人抓走郑濂,另外几个兄弟争相要入京替哥哥承罪,争来争去,最小的弟弟郑涍力排众议只身来到南京。兄弟争相入狱被传为佳话,这事情感动了朱元璋,他不但没有治罪郑家,反而给郑涍升了官。朱元璋当时就对郑濂说:"你家九世同住,孝义名冠天下,果然名不虚传,可谓天下第一家。"这很好地诠释了效忠才能两全。凭借好学的风尚和孝义的名声,从宋、元到明、清,郑义门约有173人为官,尤其是明代,出仕者达47人,官位最高者位居礼部尚书。令人惊叹的是,郑氏子孙中,竟没有一人因贪罢官。

The big clan had a very specific division of work mainly managed by the chief steward and the head was in charge of the family. The former was in charge of the clan affairs, while the latter was in charge of the domestic events. In Ming Dynasty, Zheng Lian, the chief steward of the Zheng family of Pujiang, was involved in a case of over-sighting the bribery committed by an imperial-college student who manipulated the field records. The ministry of penalty sent officials to arrest Zheng Lian, while his brothers competed to take place of him to accept punishment. The youngest brother Zheng Wei stood out at last and came to Nanjing alone. This story moved the emperor Zhu Yuanzhang so much that he didn't punish Zheng Family anymore but appointed Zheng Wei to an official position. The emperor said to Zheng Lian : "your family with nine generations under one roof is nationwide-famous for filial piety and justice. From this event, you deserve this reputation and can be named the top family in virtue". This is the best interpretation of filial piety and justice. By virtue of filial piety and justice, there cultivated 173 officials in Song, Yuan, Ming and Qing Dynasties. In the Ming Dynasty especially, there were 47 officials, the highest rank of whom was the director of the Board of Rites. The most astonishing is that no one was dismissed for corruption.

家训族规　Family Norms and Clan Regulations

"国有国法,家有家规",在宗族中家训族规就是家族成员必须遵守的行事规范。族规是宗族祖辈历代组织修订的公约,其核心是"敬宗收族"。"敬宗收族"致力于简历家族血缘关系的尊卑伦序,"收族"则寻求族人间和平共处,聚而不散。

"The country has its state laws, while the family has its domestic rules". the family norms and the clan regulations as the standards that clansmen must abide by were revised by generations. The core is to respect and maintain the authority and management of the clan. That is to say, it is to keep seniority rules and maintain peaceful coexistence for union.

宗族每年有一项最主要的活动就是祭祖。何氏宗祠建于明万历三十七年。门口的三对旗杆象征其地位与荣誉。一般在年底都有一个谢年的活动。家家户户拿出自家的贡品到宗祠去祭祖。宗族会请戏班子开春演戏,一般都是演叠八仙为主。不同宗族祭祖方式也会稍微有变化。郑义门的祭祖仪式在每年的农历2月初八,也是在宗祠里面进行。不少外地宗亲都赶来祭拜。韩国也有郑家后裔,韩国的郑姓人口多达70万,大多是华人后裔,其中郑义门一脉至少有1万3千人。他们是郑义门第六世迁徙到韩国的,其中包括大名鼎鼎的韩国现代集团创始人郑周永、郑梦准父子。

The clan holds the significant ancestral ceremony annually. The ancestral hall of He family was built in the 37th year of the Emperor Wanli of the Ming Dynasty. The three pairs of flagpoles stand for status and honor. The ceremony of inviting gods respectfully is held each year. Households take out tributes for worshiping ancestors. The clan will invite the traditional opera troupe for performance, mainly of Eight Immortals. The sacrificial activities are different slightly in clans. In terms of Zheng Family, the ancestral-worship ceremony is held in the ancestral hall on 8th day of the second lunar month annually. Plenty of kinship came for worship. There is a population of more than 700 thousand of Zheng residents, most of them are Chinese descendents. 13 thousand among them are the 6th-generation Zheng descendents who emigrated to the South Korea. In particular, Zheng

Zhouyong and Zheng Menghuai, the founder of Hyundai group, are Zheng descendents.

宗族通常出资兴建学堂,用于教育族中子弟。一般全族的家塾设在宗祠中。一般都是学生自带板凳,学生家长轮流给先生送饭。郑家的孝义教育从娃娃抓起。族人从 5 岁开始学礼,8 岁进家塾读书,12 岁出就外傅,16 岁入大学,一直读到 21 岁。郑氏宗族规定,已冠弟子在学时,每十日轮流背书,若有一次不通,则揭去头巾,三次不行则除冠。参加家务活动的青年,要努力学习办事的能力,如跟随管事人到官厅学习办理事务和处理人际关系。成年族人,每日清早要到"有序堂"听诵训诫词,每月初一、十五聆听《训诫歌》。男训主要是孝怫仁恕、积善济人,女训主要是孝顺恭敬、温和慈爱等。

The clan funds were used for building schools to educate the clan children. The family school is often set in the ancestral hall where students take seats on their own and parents deliver lunch to the teacher in turn. The education of filial piety and justice of Zheng family starts from children. The clansman starts learning rites at the age of 5, acquiring knowledge at the age of 8, going out for learning at 12, entering academic school till 21. According to Zheng Norms, the clan-approved crowned students should recite every ten days. For one failure, their hoods would be taken away, while for three failures, they would be de-crowned. For the young participating in domestic affairs, they should learn to be capable by practices such as learning from stewards to handle affairs and interpersonal relationships in offices, adults should obey and recite admonishment in "Disciplinary Hall" , and listen to "Admonishment Chants" on the 1st and 15th day every month. Males were admonished to respect seniors, to be good and forgiving, while females to respect seniors, to be kind and benevolent.

东明书院是第五世孙郑德璋创办的私塾。他规定满 16 岁的本族子弟必须就读,并聘请当时有名的学者来院执教。此后逐渐成为宗族化的书院。吴莱、宋濂等名家大儒先后来此留任主讲,为郑氏宗族培养了大量人才。

The Dongming Academy was built by the 5th-generation Zheng Dezhang as a private school. He fixed a rule that the clansmen must attend the school at 16, and he invited famous scholars to teach. This academy had gradually developed into a clan school where reputable scholars such as Wulai and Songlian retained posts and delivered lectures, which has fostered plenty of talents for Zheng family.

宗祠 Ancestral Hall

宗祠也称祠堂,是宗族最高权力的办事场所,也是供奉神主的地方。除祭祀祖先、管理公共事务外,一些族人的私事或族人间的纠纷也在此处置。此外,宗祠还肩负着扶贫济困、教化娱乐等功能。宗祠是宗族事务的核心,在族人的生活中占据着重要的地位。

The ancestral hall, the memorial temple, is the working office of the supreme power holder in the clan and also the place to worship gods. Besides worshiping ancestor and managing public affairs, handling problems or conflicts between clansmen were also undertaken here. In addition, the ancestral hall shouldered responsibilities of assisting the weak and the poor as well as cultivation and entertainment. As the center of handling affairs of the clan system, it played a significant role in the life of residents.

宗族治理的具体实践 Practices of the Clan Management

祠堂管事会依据族规行使族权,组织每年的宗族祭祖仪式,兴办家族书院推行宗族教育,执行保卫乡里、维系秩序和抚恤救济的职责,加强组内血亲的凝聚力,如今,人们依然能从金华各村落的祠堂中发现它所延续的社会功能。

The committee of the ancestral hall implemented the authorized rights accordingly, organized the annual ritual for ancestor worship, promoted the clan academies and developed the clan education, shouldered responsibilities of protecting residence, maintaining rules and regulations, and assisting the disadvantaged and relieving the needed so as to enhance and strengthen the clan union. Till now, it is still known to us of the social functions from the ancestral halls in villages of Jinhua.

祠堂是供奉和祭祀祖先的场所。宗族管事会每年组织并举办数次祭祖仪式,族中成年男性方可参加。通过分房派献礼、祭典等活动程序,强化宗族内成员间的联系和对血缘族亲的认同。

The ancestral hall is for worshiping ancestors. The committee of the clan stewards hold annual ancestor-worshiping ceremonies that require only male adults to participate in. It is to strengthen the relationship between clansmen as well as to stabilize recognition of self-identity in the clan.

耕读传家　Farming and Reading

耕田以立性命,读书以立高德,成为乡村社会耕读传家的教育理念。宗族出资兴建学堂,用于教育族中子弟。家塾通常设在宗祠,也有一些有实力的家族在家中延请名师或兴建私塾。勤耕苦读、忠义孝悌等德行教育由此得以代代相传。

That farming makes a living and reading makes a virtue has become a concept of education in villages. The clan funded schools to educate the clan children. Some family schools were often set in the ancestral halls while some private schools were favored by certain wealthy families who employed famous teachers for education. It is through the clan education that the doctrines such as diligent farming and reading, loyalty, filial piety and fraternal duty could be handed down from to generation.

保卫乡里　Protection of Neighborhood

特殊时期,宗族管事与宗祠管事会往往肩负保护族群、守卫乡里的职责。一旦灾祸发生,管事们会召集族人在宗祠中议事,并以全族名义维护地方安全。平时则通过族规、巡查等方式,防范灾害发生,提高应对灾害的能力。

Clan stewards and the committee were expected to shoulder responsibilities of protecting the clan and residence in certain special circumstances. Once disasters befell, stewards would sum up clansmen to discuss countermeasures in order to protect their residence in terms of the whole clan system, while in ordinary times, they made precautions against disasters through ways of rules and inspections.

水龙会是民间消防组织,由村中族长或者辈分较高的长辈出面组织,村中青年自愿组成。村民自筹资金或族中出资购置水龙、水桶,建水龙屋。村中一旦失火,村民鸣锣呼救,水龙会会员不论农活多忙,也不管是本村还是邻村都要参加灭火。

The hoses association as a civil fire-fighting organization, is organized by the chief steward or the seniors and undertaken by volunteering young people. Villages self-funded hoses, buckets and construction of hose houses. Once the village was caught in fire, villagers would strike gongs for help, the association members, no matter how busy they were and no matter where they were from (local villagers or neighboring villagers), should participate in fire fighting.

浦江郑宅水龙会 Pujiang Zheng's Fire Fighting Association

早在 1461 年浦江郑宅就有了水龙会,共有水龙会 8 支,分别为枣元、上郑、五房、丰产、冷水、东明、后溪、东庄。各村派专人分管水龙会事务,定措施保证其稳定的资金来源。每年农历八月初一,浦江郑宅、岩头等乡镇都要举办"赛水龙"。最初比拼水龙会实力的赛事逐渐成为民俗节日传承至今。这天,各村会把"水龙"拉到村口水塘边试车。

As early as 1461, there was a fire-fighting association with 8 branches in Zaoyuan, Shangzheng, Wufang, Fengchan, Lengshui, Dongming, Houxi and Dongzhuang in Zheng's residence of Pujiang. Each village dispatched a specially-assigned person in charge of fire-fighting affairs and measures to maintain a stable funds. On the 1st day of the eighth lunar month, villages such as Zheng's residence of Pujiang and Yantou would hold "competition in fire fighting" that has been developed into a folk festival now. On that day, each village would pull the cart along the pond at the village entrance for a trial.

维系秩序　Order maintaining

族规规定,族人必须恪守道德伦理规范,禁止危害公共利益,否则处罚严厉。一旦族人违反家规,宗族管事会以"开大宗祠"的办法予以惩治。奖赏也是宗族维持秩序的一种方式,宗族会为守孝持节的族人建祠立坊以示表彰。

According to the clan rules, clansmen must abide by moral and ethical norms. It is forbidden to endanger the public interests. Otherwise, he or she would be punished severely. Once anyone violated rules, the clan would mete out punishment to him by a solemn disciplinary meeting in the ancestral hall. Besides rules of punishment, the clan adopted rules of reward to maintain the balance. They would establish memorial temples or archways for rewarding those of filial piety or chastity.

浦江郑宅郑氏宗族族规严苛,一旦有人触犯,就要"开大宗祠",总管事端坐于正堂,管事会召集全体族人在堂前两侧旁听。违反家规者罚跪于堂前,只要比他大一岁,就要拜30次。如果还不知悔改,就要打板子。再不悔过则除族籍并送官府惩治。若悔改,三年后复归宗族。《郑氏规范》中数条警示子孙"莫伸手"的家规,如果有贪污,就在宗谱里面除名,死后牌位也不能入祠堂。

The Zheng family of Pujiang had harsh rules and whoever violated the rules would be punished in the ancestral hall. The chief steward sat straightly in the main hall, while the other clansmen audited on either side of the hall. For these who violated rules, they should kowtow for 30 times. If they were impenitent later, they should be thrashed by birches. But if they were still stubborn and impenitent at last, they should be taken to the feudal government for more severe punishment. If they repented and minded their ways, they could return to the clan. According to *Zheng's Norms*, all the decedents should not long for and take possessions of others. Once they committed corruption, they would be removed from the genealogy, and their memorial tablet will not be placed in the ancestral hall.

抚恤救济　Pensions and Relief Funds

宗族肩负着赡养族人的职责,管事会利用族产以不同方式对族内孤儿、老人提供帮助,设置义田、义庄等以备灾荒。

The clan shoulders responsibilities of supporting clansmen. The committee utilized possessions to assist orphans and elders as well as to spare free fields and houses as reliefs against disasters.

《郑氏规范》中第 15 条:身为家长以诚待下,讲话不可以随便,行动不可以妄为。希望家长行事能符合古人以身作则之意。临事之际,不要在细节问题上过于计较,也不要糊涂待事。决断时要大度,爱护家庭跟爱护自己的身体一样。第 134 条:我家既然旌表为孝义家门,家族的风气和追求的目标无非是要行积善之事。子孙都应当深刻领会,不得任意妄为,对乡亲作威作福,不得谋划胁迫他人钱财、侵犯他人产业,不要成为祖宗积德的败类。违者以不孝论。

Zheng Family Norms-item 15: a head of the family, you should not talk and behave deliberately and keep merits of ancestors to set himself an example. Don't be too picky on details when handling matters, don't be muddled when dealing with problems, be magnanimous when making decisions, cherish family the same as your own body. Item 134: since we are a clan of filial piety and brotherhood, we are in pursuit of being good. All the descendants should understand the profound pursuit, don't be reckless, don't roughshod over locals, don't conspire and threaten others' possessions, don't infringe upon others' properties, don't degenerate the clan, whoever violate the above will be punished in terms of impiety.

所以说宗族实际上就是一个完整的小社会。宗族内所受的教化对整个社会也起到了一定作用。

The clan is in effect a complete mini society where the cultivation has played a role in the whole society.

节庆——宗教的节庆与信仰 Festivals: Religious Festivals and Beliefs
在以农业为主导的社会,风调雨顺是人们共同的愿望。人们相信通过各种虔诚的仪式,如迎龙灯、攀台阁、斗牛等,能让各方神明驱散邪气,佑护一方。宗祠前的广场成为人们娱神祭祀的主要场所。在宗族管事会的安排下,村民们各司其职、共同参与,分享节日的快乐与祝福,各地地方信仰和节庆礼俗也借此传承至今。

In the agriculture-oriented society, folks shared the same blessing of favorable weathers. It was believed that the pious rituals such as ushering dragon-lantern, climbing high and bullfighting could dispel evils and protect them. The square in front of the ancestral hall was mainly used for entertainment and god-worship. According to the management of the clan committee, folks with respective duties coparticipate and enjoy joy and blessings in festivals. Local beliefs and festivals were thus passed down from age to age.

第二节　主要古村落简介　Major Ancient Villages

琐园村①　Suoyuan Village

琐园村位于金华市东郊,澧浦镇北一千米处。琐园村周围分布着七座山包,靠北有一湖,形成了天然的"七星拱月"星象地理,有专家称之为中国古代生态建筑的经典遗产。琐园村现有460几户,人口1 200多人。严、俞、徐等为大姓,而第一大姓严氏是严子陵的后代。

Located in the east of Jinhua, Suoyuan Village is 1 km away from the north of Li Pu Town. Surrounded by seven mountains and with a lake in the north, the astrological geography "Seven Stars Arched Around the Moon" was formed naturally. Some experts called it the classical heritage of Chinese Ancient Ecological Construction. Now Suoyuan Village has over 460 houses and 1 200 people. Their main surnames are Yan, Yu, Xu, among which the people of the family name Yan are later generations of Yan Ziling.

琐园村的一绝是庞大的明清古建筑群。据严氏家谱记载,清朝祖族严子陵第五十一世严必胜率兵平定两广匪乱有功，皇帝诏允为官，他在家乡琐园盖了十八座雕梁画栋的厅堂。历经岁月风雨，现保存的古建筑有旌节石牌坊、严氏宗祠、务本堂、怀德堂、聚义厅等明末清初堂屋十六座，是金华规模最大的古建筑群之一。这些厅堂建筑结构、艺术风格各不相同，都极具江南古民居的典型特色。

The large group of constructions built in Ming and Qing Dynasties is marvelous. According to the Genealogy of Yan, Yan Bisheng (the 51st generation of Yan Ziling) was awarded an official by the Qing Emperor for his contribution in the war against the rebel armies of Guangdong and Guangxi. Then he built 18 halls with carved girders and painted beams. Now preserved ancient buildings like Jingjie Stone Arch, Yan Ancestral Hall, Wuben Hall, Huaide Hall, Juyi ting 16 rooms can be dated back to the late Ming Dynasty, which is one of the largest scale ancient construction groups in Jinhua. Being varied in construction structures and art styles, these halls are typical representatives of ancient residence in the south area of the Yangtze River.

农耕文化是指由农民在长期农业生产中形成的一种风俗文化，以为农业服务和农民自身娱乐为中心。农业最早在中原地区兴起。中原农耕文化包含了众多特色耕作技术和科学发明。琐园村展现的部分农业生产工具为金华农耕文化提供了实物证据。如今随着机械化程度的提高，靠人力耕作的时代已基本结束，原始农具也完成了它的历史使命，成为传承农耕文化的历史记忆。

Farming culture is a kind of custom formed by farmers in the long-term agricultural production, which is centered with agricultural service and farmers' own entertainment. Agriculture was first founded in the Central Plains region. The farming culture of the Central Plains contains a number of characteristic farming techniques and scientific inventions. Part of the agricultural production tools displayed in Suoyuan Village give evidence to Jinhua farming culture. Now, with the increasing mechanization, the farming era of human comes to an end. The primitive farming tools have completed their mission, becoming a historical memory of the farming culture.

寺平村^②　Siping Village

寺平村东距汤溪镇 6 千米,原有厅堂 24 座,现保存较完整的还有 8 座。厅堂占地面积 6000 平方米,古民居 2.2 万多平方米。这些古建筑融入了粉墙、青瓦、马头墙、高脊飞檐等徽派建筑的元素,并以数以万计的精美砖雕赢得了"中国最美的砖雕在寺平"的美誉。

Siping Village is 6 kilometers away from Tangxi Town in the east. There were 24 halls of celebrity originally, while eight of them are well-preserved today. The total area of these halls is 6000 ㎡, and the traditional residential building covers an area of 22,000 ㎡. These ancient buildings contain elements of Huizhou style, such as whitewashed wall, gray tile, horse-head wall and high ridge with overhanging eaves. With tens of thousands of exquisite brick carvings, Siping wins a reputation of "The most beautiful brick carving of China is in Siping" .

据《戴氏宗谱》记载,寺平村的先人们没有按照坐北朝南的常规来选址,而是因地制宜,以近临的东边七座山丘做屏障,把七座山丘寓意成天体的东方七宿,并将村基设计成半个月亮的形状,同时,在村庄宗祠百顺堂前有个半月形的水塘名叫"月湖",从而形成"七星伴月"、坐东朝西、依山面水的村落格局。同时,村里的道路规划和主要厅堂布局也是按照"七星"的方位来布局的。寺平村主要厅堂的大门基本上都是朝西或朝南方向开的,以朝西方向为主,和村庄的布局和朝向是相呼应的。

According to the well-preserved *Genealogy of Dai's Family*, the ancestors of Siping village selected the site according to the circumstances rather than following the conventional rule of facing south. Using seven hills in the nearby east as a barrier, they considered them as the seven oriental constellations and designed the base of Siping in the shape of a half moon. Meanwhile, in front of the Baishun Hall (the ancestral hall of the village) lies a half-moon pond called "Moon Lake" , thus forming a layout of "Seven

Stars Around Moon",which is facing west, surrounded by mountains and water. Also, the planning of the road and the layout of the main halls were managed in the same way. Most of gates the primary halls are facing west or south, mainly west, which correspond to the layout and orientations of the village.

寺平村的七座主要厅堂对应着北斗七星,其中安乐寺对应北斗七星的北斗勺子外沿的第一星即天枢星,代表着力量;其顺堂对应第二星天璇星,代表着智慧;立本堂对应第三星天玑星,代表着勇气;崇德堂对应第四星天权星,代表着爱情;崇厚堂对应玉衡星,代表着幸福;敦睦堂对应开阳星,代表着远离灾祸;百顺堂对应着北斗勺柄的摇光星,代表着重生后的圆满。这七座厅堂的建造上应星宿,下合地势,内含意蕴,神奇地环绕成北斗七星的图案,伴着月亮在人间的投影月湖,构成了寺平古村最为奇妙的自然人文景观。

The seven main halls of Siping Village correspond to seven stars of the Big Dipper, corresponding to the first star Dubhe, Anle Temple represents strength; corresponding to the second Merak, Qishun Hall represents wisdom; corresponding to the third Phecda, Liben Hall represents courage; corresponding to the forth Megrez, Chongde Hall represents love; corresponding to the fifth Alioth, Chonghou Hall represents happiness; corresponding to the sixth Mizar, Dunmu Hall represents safety, corresponding to the last Alkaid, Baishun Hall represents satisfaction after rebirth. Agreeing to the constellation and the terrain and with the profound meanings, they magically form the image of the Big Dipper with the moon shade in the "Moon Lake". All these made the most marvelous nature wonders and human landscapes in Siping.

根雕起源于中国,根艺家对天然的树根依性造势,突出自然美与人的技巧相结合,雕刻出既实用又可欣赏的工艺品。婺城根雕以郑宗均为代表,他继承了前人根雕艺术的精华,经过自己的努力和创新,形成了自己独特的风格。

Originated in China, Root carving artists undertake innovations according to the shape of natural roots and emphasize on the combination of the natural beauty with human techniques, producing art works with both practicability and appreciation. The representative of Wucheng Root carving is Zheng Zongjun. He inherited the essence of the predecessors and formed a unique style of his own during years of work and innovation.

汤溪棕编又称"棕榈叶艺编",是土色土香的传统民间绝技。棕榈叶艺编是用新鲜棕榈叶通过剪、缠、绕、拉等手法编织制作,与传承至今的制作技艺基本上一致。

Tangxi Zongbian, also called "Palm Fronds Weaving Art", is a unique traditional folk techniques. Palm Fronds Weaving Art is manufactured with fresh palm fronds by cutting, twining, twisting, pulling, which is almost the same as the processing used today.

茶罐窑,主料为白石泥,也称观音土,是从水塘里挖出的一种特殊的软泥。制作时配以清水塑型。茶罐窑的制作非常复杂,有十几道工序,另外根据当天制作时的天气状况不同,各个工序的时间等都需要有所改变。

The main ingredient is white clay, also called "Guanyin Tu", which is a special soft mud in the pond. It is to use pure water to make the shape, while making teapot kiln is complicated as it needs more than ten processes. What's more, different weather conditions lead to different humidity of the mud, which requires different time for each process.

俞源村[③]　Yuyuan Village

明代俞源旱涝交替,常发瘟疫,民不聊生。国师刘伯温好堪舆之学,上通天文,下晓地理,设计并指挥改村口直溪为曲溪,以溪流为阴阳鱼界线设立太极图。经测量太极图直径为 320 米,面积 8 公顷。同时,设计了村庄建筑的星象,八卦布局。

Striken by droughts, floods and plague, Yuyuan people in the Ming Dynasty suffered a lot. The national consultant Liu Bowen, who was good at Feng Shui and had a rich knowledge of everything redesigned the straight river at the gate of the village into a bent one. He set the stream as the boundary of Yin and Yang, thus forming a Tai Chi chart. The diameter of Tai Chi is 320 meters, covering an area of 8 hectares. At the same time, he made the astrology of the village construction layout.

俞源太极星象村坐落在浙江省武义县西南部，距县城 20 千米。现存宋元明清古建筑 1027 间。古建筑内木雕、砖雕、石雕精致，巧夺天工。在村口有占地 8 公顷的巨型太极图。村中布有七星塘、七星井。俞源村文化底蕴深厚，人文景观与自然景观密切融合，是古生态"天人合一"的经典遗存，是寻古探秘休闲的旅游胜地。

Yu Yuan Tai Chi astrology village is located in the southwest of Wuyi County, Zhejiang Province, which is 20 km from the county. There exist 1027 rooms of the Ming and Qing ancient buildings. Delicate wood, brick and stone carvings decorate the ancient buildings well. At the gate of the village lies a huge Tai Chi with an area of 8 hectares. The village is set with "Seven stars pond"and "Seven Stars Well". With a rich culture background and well-mixed human landscapes with natural scenes, Yuyuan is a classical remain of the paleoecologic unity as well as a marvelous place to explore a mystery.

村周十一道山岗与太极阴阳鱼构成天体黄道十二宫，八卦形排列的 28 座堂楼，对应星象二十八宿，七星塘、七星井呈北斗星状分布，俞氏宗祠正好位于七星斗内。

The eleven hills around the village together with the Tai Chi Yin Yang pond formed the Celestial Zodiac. The 28 buildings arranged in the shape of Eight Diagrams correspond to the lunar mansions. The "Seven-star pond" and the "Seven- Star Well" are distributed in the Big Dipper, where the Ancestral Hall of Yu Family is located.

俞源太极星象村现存古建筑 1072 间，占地 3.4 万平方米，有民居、宗祠、店铺、庙宇、书馆等。古建筑体量大，做工精致，古屋、古桥保存完好，墙上壁画保存完好，木雕、砖雕、石雕精细，巧夺天工，将功能与艺术、实用与美化很好地结合在一起,并与建筑主体结构完美地融合起来,独具江南风格。始建于南宋的洞主庙,是远近闻名的圆梦胜地。每年的"梦圆节",前来许愿的游客络绎不绝。

Filled with houses, temples, shops, temples, libraries and so on, Yu Yuan Tai Chi astrology village now exists 1072 rooms of old buildings, covering an area of 34,000 m². The large number of exquisite ancient constructions, well-preserved historic houses, bridges and wall paintings as well as the delicate wood, brick and stone carvings show a good combination of the function and art, also the unite of practicability and beauty. All these are perfectly mixed together with the main buildings, showing a unique style of its own. Dated back to the Southern Song Dynasty, the Dongzhu Temple was famous for realizing the dreams. Crowds of people comes to the temple for a good luck every year when the Dream Day arrives.

诸葛八卦村[④]　Zhuge Eight-Diagram Village

诸葛利的儿子诸葛青于北宋天禧二年(公元 1018 年)迁居兰溪,诸葛青的一个儿子诸葛承载在兰溪传了十代,到诸葛大狮举家迁到高隆(即诸葛八卦村)。因诸葛承载这一系诸葛家族秉承先祖诸葛亮的教导,"不为良相,便为良医",他们精心经营中医药业,所制良药,畅销大江南北,财富积累不少,人丁最为兴旺。诸葛村的大经堂(中药展览馆),便是诸葛承载家族在中医药业成就的集中展示。

Zhuge Qing (the son of Zhuge Li) moved to Lanxi in the Tianxi Period of the Northern Song Dynasty (1018 A.D.). Zhuge Chengzai (the son of Zhuge Qing) had ten generations in Lanxi. Later, Zhuge Dashi moved the whole family to Gaolong, where now is Zhuge Eight-Diagram village. Zhuge Chengzai and his posterity followed the instructions being a good doctor if not a good minister, which was said by Zhuge Liang, they devoted in running Chinese Medicine. As their products were popular all over the country, the family made a fortune and became the most prospered branch. The achievement of Zhuge Chengzai Family in Chinese Medicine is displayed in the Dajing Hall (Chinese Medicine Exhibition Hall).

诸葛大狮运用自己学到的风水学知识，按九宫八卦构思，精心设计了整个八卦村的布局：以钟池为核心，八条小巷向外辐射，形成内八卦，妙的是村外刚好有八座小山，形成环抱之势，构成外八卦。村内房屋分布在八条小巷，虽然历经几百年岁月，人丁兴旺，屋子越盖越多，但是九宫八卦的总体布局一直不变。

Using what he had learned about Feng Shui, Zhuge Dashi delicately desig-ned the layout of the village according to the conception of Protective Talisman Charts. Centered with the Zhong Lake, the eight alleys stretch out and form an internal Eight Diagram. What's more, the surrounding of the eight mountains outside the village shape the external Eight Diagram. More and more houses stand in the eight alleys through hundreds of years with a fixed layout of Protective Talisman Charts.

大公堂，位于村的中心，坐北朝南。据说是江南地区唯一仅存的诸葛亮纪念堂。堂内壁上绘有有关诸葛亮的故事壁画。

Dagong Hall, located in the center of the village, faces the south. It is said to be the only memorial hall of Zhuge Liang in the south region of Yangtz River. The famous historical stories of Zhuge Liang were painted on the wall of the memorial hall.

居民住宅，诸葛村的大部分住宅都是造在起伏的山坡上，从前到后逐渐升高，叫作"步步高"。

Residential houses are mostly built on fluctuating hills, which start from the front to the back, meaning promotion in position.

丞相祠堂，是为纪念诸葛亮而修建的，坐东朝西，平面按"回"字形布局，有屋 52 间，由门厅、中庭、庑廊、钟鼓楼和享堂组成。

Prime Minister (in ancient China) Hall, which is built in honor of Zhuge Liang, lays out according to the Chinese character "回"and faces west. Consisting of the vestibule, atrium,veranda, tower and sacrificial hall, the Prime Minister Hall has a total of 52 rooms.

钟池,位于诸葛村的中心,在大公堂正前面,它的边上是一块与它逆对称的陆地,村民用以晒场之用。空地和钟池正呈阴阳太极图形。

Zhong Lake lays in the middle of the village, right in front of the Dagong Hall, beside which is an inverse symmetry land used as a bleachery by villagers. The land and the lake form exactly a Tai Chi Chart.

农坊馆,诸葛村的农坊馆里面有作板、古老的织布机、碾坊、碾盘、油坊、炒锅、小手磨等。可以感受诸葛亮历代后裔宁静淡泊的村居生活和积极进取的民俗风情。

Farming and Textile House in the village has tools like board, old loom, grain mill, grinding base, oil mill, pan, small hand mill and so on. On seeing these, we can feel the peaceful life and the positive customs of the villagers.

诸葛村的龙灯属于"桥灯",又称"板凳龙",分"龙头"和"灯桥"两部分。龙头用篾条扎成架子,外面湖上棉纸,再配以多种饰品;"灯桥"是由几十桥,多的由一百五六十桥桥灯连接而成,在长约一米左右的桥板上扎三盏花灯,称为"一桥灯"。灯桥的最后有一个长约一米多的,由篾扎纸糊的龙尾。

Bench Dragon consists of "dragon head " and "lantern bridge". Dragon lantern in Zhuge Village is called "bridge lantern" , also known as "bench dragon". As for the head of the dragon, it uses bamboo strip to make a profile, uses cotton paper to wrap the profile outside, and finally decorates with accessories. "Lantern Bench" is connected by a dozen or about 150-160 benches. Each one-meter bench has three lanterns, thus is called "one bridge lantern". At the end of the lantern bench there is a dragon tail made by the same material as the head.

注释：

① Source:https://baike.baidu.com/item/%E7%90%90%E5%9B%AD%E6%9D%91/1635540?fr=aladdin 中文有修改。

② Source:https://baike.baidu.com/item/%E5%AF%BA%E5%B9%B

3%E6%9D%91 中文有修改。

③ Source: https://baike.baidu.com/item/%E4%BF%9E%E6%BA%90%E6%9D%91 中文有修改。

④ Source: https://baike.baidu.com/item/%E8%AF%B8%E8%91%9B%E5%85%AB%E5%8D%A6%E6%9D%91 中文有修改。